BUSINESS CHAMELEON

For a complete list of Management Books 2000 titles,
visit our web-site on http://www.mb2000.com

BUSINESS CHAMELEON

The Art of Achieving Success in Business Abroad

Ron Roet and Diana Beaver

2000

Also by Diana Beaver

NLP for Lazy Learning (Vega Books)
Easy Being: Making Life as Simple and as Much Fun as Possible (The Useful Book Company)

First published in 2003 by Management Books 2000 Ltd
Forge House, Limes Road
Kemble, Cirencester
Gloucestershire, GL7 6AD, UK
Tel: 0044 (0) 1285 771441/2
Fax: 0044 (0) 1285 771055
E-mail: m.b.2000@virgin.net
Web: mb2000.com

Printed and bound in Great Britain by Biddles, Guildford

British Library Cataloguing in Publication Data is available
ISBN 1-85252-429-4

Foreword

Whilst supervising a recent MBA Dissertation at Henley Management College, my candidate sent me an e-mail asking if it was permissible to quote from an as yet unpublished book. He enthusiastically described to me the Cultural Auras Theory (that you will read about in this publication) he had discovered and was keen to introduce the concept in his research focusing on the cultural challenges of management in China. Naturally, it was my duty to investigate this new approach to cultural analysis and this brought me into contact with the authors, Ron Roet and Diana Beaver.

Whilst not an NLP (Neuro-Linguistic Programming) expert, I had worked alongside many practitioners in this field to understand the power of this approach to rapport-building and influencing. These two key interpersonal competencies are particularly relevant to developing what I term 'cultural fluency' yet there had been few credible attempts to link cross-cultural capabilities with NLP skills. Through this book, Diana and Ron have addressed this vacuum using their Cultural Auras Theory to help the reader develop a successful approach to winning business in culturally-diverse markets.

Written in a relaxed, non-academic style, 'Business Chameleon' takes us on a meandering path of cultural education and enlightenment, highlighting important features of inter-cultural relationships using numerous personal anecdotes and travellers' tales. This is a book that draws heavily on the authors' varied experiences and backgrounds and hence has a very pragmatic approach to the inevitable situations most international business people will face.

A chameleon is an apt creature to capture the essence of fluency across cultures. Whilst you do not give up your individual framework of who you are, it may be necessary to change your colour scheme according to different environments.

Cultures being likened to a series of 'auras' through which one achieves relationship success across the globe is inspiring. 'Auras' conjure up Saturn-like images of hazy, colourful and variable layers of matter. Sometimes this matter is dense, sometimes it is loose, and sometimes it is intangible. This is how culture confronts us in the real world and 'Business Chameleon' will help you to find your way through these auras in pursuit of effective cross-cultural relationships.

David Rees
Visiting Faculty, Henley Management College
and Director, Cultural Fluency Ltd

May 2003

This one's for my friend, teacher and mentor, Robert Dilts, who creates a truly international world in Santa Cruz, Ca, where one makes friends whom one keeps for life.

And also for my womenfolk, Ming and Charlie, with my love.

DB

I dedicate this book to my wife, Monique, and our children, Kevin, Menno and Celine, all a tremendous source of inspiration.

RR

Acknowledgements

I would like to acknowledge the many people I have met around the world who were the source of my inspiration. Without them this book would never have been written.

I also would like to thank my wife, Monique for coping with me during the writing of this book and for her exceptional ideas.

I would like to thank Diana for the many hours we have spent together writing and debating. She is an inspiration to mankind.

I especially need to mention and thank Tom Roland for his positive and excellent criticism, Joachim Limberg for his priceless input, David Rees for writing the foreword and his brilliant suggestions, James Alexander, our editor and publisher for his enthusiasm.

Furthermore I would like to thank Mel Petrie, Terry Noble, Terry Sargeant, Phil Lowe, Bob Johns, Ludo Dillen, Dr Salim Aziz, Peel Holroyd and many others for their motivation.

RR

I would like to thank all those people from around the world who have gathered us into their cultures, made us so welcome and taught us so much; my husband Philip who has been endlessly patient, and who also kept the computer in order and taught it and me to do complicated things; Ron, for his wisdom, entertainment and patience; and Geoffrey and Tecla Adams for introducing me to Ron – without them this book would never have happened.

I must also acknowledge the BNI (Business Network International) connections, without whom we would never have met David Rees, and all my students, clients, friends and colleagues in the NLP world, from whom I have learned so much, especially (in order of acquaintance) John Grinder, Judith DeLozier, Robert Dilts, the late Todd Epstein, Stephen Gilligan and Richard Bandler. I hope I have given them credit, where credit is due and, if not, that they will forgive me.

DB

The Business Chameleon

The Art of Achieving Success in Business Abroad

Contents

Introduction

With communication and travel becoming faster and easier day by day, there appears to be no excuse for not operating world-wide. So what stops us? How is it that these foreigners don't jump at the chance of doing business with us?

We only have to think of some of the emails we get, with no salutation and precious little punctuation, because everyone's in such a hurry; or the offices where people communicate by email, rather than cross the room to talk to each other, to realise that, while the speed of our communication has increased, the quality of that communication has deteriorated. And effective communication is the be-all and end-all of successful business – whether it be at home or abroad. The only difference between doing business at home and abroad is that, abroad, they think differently.

To this end, the first magic word is 'culture'. We think the way we think because of *our* culture; foreigners think in their way because of *their* culture. And, the moment we forget this simple fact, we can find ourselves in trouble. As an example, there is the sad story of two companies, one American and the other German, getting together to discuss a project: *the Americans were trying to be friendly, but the Germans interpreted this as frivolous; the Germans applied their critical minds to the project, but the Americans interpreted this as coldness and lack of interest. The meeting over, they shook hands, made their farewells, and that was the end of the project.* Each race was simply behaving according to its culture, and both decided that the others were not the sort of people they wanted to do business with.

This book is the result of the authors meeting at a party and finding ourselves bemoaning incidents like the above; we discovered that we had both been wanting for years to write a book about cross-cultural misunderstandings. Ron was developing his Cultural Auras Theory (hereinafter referred to as CAT) as a result of more than 20 years' experience of international business in many different cultures; and Diana was using Neuro-Linguistic Programming (hereinafter referred to as NLP), to create a structure for cross-cultural understanding because, as we saw above, the main problem with culture is that it is so deeply ingrained in us that we may be completely unaware of how much it influences us. It may never cross our minds that ours is not 'the one right way' of doing things.

The second magic word is 'relationships'. While we would agree that the bottom line is important, and that unless we do our sums right, our business could find itself in trouble, the accountants seem to have forgotten the simple fact that, wherever we are in the world, people buy people – rather than their products; so it's the relationship that counts.

Business is an art, rather than a science. This book is about intangible assets, which can't be measured, and without which it cannot work.

CAT is new, exciting and simple. It provides us with a visual structure of how and when relationships can be formed with people from different cultures. NLP is also exciting and simple; it has been going since the '60s. There is nothing new in NLP, it is just the study of the structure of excellence; in other words, *how do people do what they do so well?* And, more importantly, *how do they think about what they are doing?*

Ron has been doing business successfully around the world since 1979, without knowing anything about NLP. But, when we analyse the way he works and the way his thinks about it, we discover that it is pure NLP. If you ask assorted NL-People how they describe NLP, you will probably get different answers: Robert Dilts, of the NLP University in Santa Cruz, California, says: 'if it works, it's NLP, if it doesn't, it isn't', and Diana describes it as 'applying objectivity (which is the way we are supposed to think), to subjectivity (which is the way we really think – because we're humans, rather than robots)'. NLP is based on a series of presuppositions, things we presuppose before applying ourselves to any problem. Nobody would claim that any of these presuppositions is true – they simply provide us with a useful structure of thinking, which can be applied to any problem.

Neuro-Linguistic Programming is a terrible name, and almost guaranteed to scare off all but the most curious. However, it does describe what it is all about.

Neuro refers to the brain/body connection: for centuries, 'they' have tried to make us behave logically, and not to allow emotions to interfere with our thinking; but humans are subjective beings, and we are each a system. If we stick a pin into you, your brain is going to know about it; and, when someone tells you you're wonderful, your body is going to feel it.

Linguistic refers to the language we use to describe our experiences, and how we are processing our thinking: *'the way I see it ...'* demonstrates that the person is interpreting events through pictures in his or her mind's eye; whereas *'what I'm hearing ...'* tells us that he or she is interpreting everything through sounds; and when someone says *'my feeling is ...'*, we pick up that they are checking everything against their feelings.

Programming relates to the programs that we run to make our lives simpler; in other words, we don't have to think how to get out of bed in the morning, or how to clean our teeth, or how to walk; we just run the program, and do it. Most of our programs are highly efficient, but some of them might not be useful – like panicking at the thought of a spider, giving a presentation, picking up the telephone to make a cold call, and so on.

Richard Bandler (who created this utterly simple way of working out how people are thinking, so that you can tune into them) describes how it got its dreadful name: he was stopped for speeding and the policeman asked what his occupation was. While one half of his brain was wondering what on earth his occupation had to do with anything, the other half was reminding him that this guy was armed. As yet he had no name for what he was doing, so he cast his eye frantically round the car in search of inspiration – and saw a book on Neurology, and book on Linguistics and a book on Computer Programming. 'I am a Neuro-Linguistic Programmer', he announced. And the policeman was, apparently, most impressed.

Some years ago, Diana did an interesting survey of businesses large and small, asking just one question: *'what stops life at work from being as simple, as productive, as effective, as fulfilling and as much fun as you'd like it to be'*, and 95% of the answers came under the heading of **'Other People'**: bosses, staff, customers and so on.

From the linguistic point of view, we talk about making friends, creating a relationship, building bridges, forging links, and all these concepts imply doing something. We can't just sit back and expect a relationship to blossom – it requires some action on our part: we need to prepare the ground, sow the seed and nurture its growth.

This book not only gives you ideas about *what* to do, more importantly, it also tells you *how* to do it, and *why* you need to do it. With the combination of CAT and NLP, our aim is to provide you with the equipment to:

- bridge the cultural gaps you'll find when doing business around the globe
- analyse with ease the differences in the way business is done, according to whatever culture you find yourself in

- substantially improve your success rate in the world market
- create sound relationships with people, with whom you can continue to do business for years to come.

Some of what you find here may seem obvious; some of it you will have forgotten that you knew, and some may seem unusual. We're all different, and we all do things in different ways. With the information you find here, you can create your own map of how to turn apparent deals into real business.

All we ask from you is that you open your mind, stretch your imagination and experiment with the ideas. If something we suggest seems impossible, test it out and see what happens. The more we expand our thinking, the more solutions become available to us.

Use and develop everything you find, and have fun, as you explore the deeper structure of business relationships.

So, who are we, and what qualifications do we have to expound our theories to you?

Ron is Dutch by birth – he was educated in Belgium; his BSc is from Reading University and his MSc from Antwerp. Since 1979, he has been travelling world-wide on business, so he has enormous experience of working successfully in different cultures. He has developed his Cultural Auras Theory so that you can not only learn about what possible cultural barriers might exist between you and business colleagues from other parts of the world, but also see at a glance how to benefit from the knowledge it gives you.

Diana is an NLP author, broadcaster, consultant and trainer, who works in any area that grabs her interest – particularly in business, education, sport and health. She is Irish by birth, was brought up in England and has also lived and worked in France, various parts of Germany, Northern Ireland and Wales. As an Irishwoman, she likes to do things the easy way – as you will discover from her earlier books: *NLP for Lazy Learning* (Vega Books) and *Easy Being: Making Life as Simple and as much Fun as Possible* (The Useful Book Company).

International negotiations – a cautionary tale

Negotiations and discussing business with other cultures – or even selling a product abroad – can go dramatically wrong as we all know and have experienced.

We only have to look objectively at what happened recently at the United Nations Security Council with resolution 1441.

We take this example because it illustrates dramatically what can go wrong in negotiations – we are not looking at the politics involved. The resolution was pretty vague and there was ample room for interpretation.

The first problem is that it was drafted in one language and then translated into many others. Consequently, the interpretation and perception differed significantly from one nation to another or even from one person to another.

Everyone agreed upon one major issue – the removal of the regime in Iraq. What they did not agree upon was the manner in which this was going to be executed.

The latter caused irritation between the negotiators concerned with major consequences as we all have observed.

The questions we can pose are:

1. Did everyone in the UN Security Council understand resolution 1441?
2. Was there too much freedom for interpretation?
3. Did they explain the decision-taking process and the timing of it?
4. Did they understand how the decision process works within the different countries represented at the UN Security Council and who makes those decisions?
5. Was there sufficient information regarding the regime in Iraq to decide one way or another?
6. Was there direct interaction between the negotiators and the regime in Iraq in order to take the decisions they took?

The power in business and in negotiations is primarily the sound understanding of the nature of the products/service/idea one is to sell and the way the buyers perceive this. As with chess, the more one knows about the possible moves one's opponent can make and how his or her mind works, the greater the chance of winning the game.

1

If We Always Do
What We've Always Done ...

The Chameleon
The most fascinating thing about this creature is that it can adapt to its surroundings. Another attribute is that its eyes are on 'turrets', so that, while it can be aware of what is going on all around it at all times, it can also focus its eyes forwards to produce stereoscopic vision when the opportunity arises for achieving its goals. Thirdly, the ancients believed that it lived on air: and we find this an appropriate metaphor for the intangible assets we are going to study in this book. These intangible assets are things you have always known about, but which have been ignored (or even beaten out of people) in the world of modern business.

If we want to work with the powerful magic required for doing business abroad, that is to create relationships within different cultures, we need to be adaptable; we need to be aware at all times of what is going on around us, as well as to be able to focus when the time is right, and we need the intangible assets we will be discussing throughout the book.

How often have you gone to a business meeting knowing that your product was good, your price was competitive and your company was sound. You made your presentation, the audience smiled, nodded and agreed with whatever you had to say, and you went home happily to report your success – but you didn't get the business?

If we always do what we've always done, then we'll always get what we've always got. In other words, if what we're doing isn't working, then it's time to do something different. This is what this book is about: giving you some different ways of thinking, and some different things to do – to bring you the success that you deserve.

To start off with, let's consider what business is about, and why we do it. There's the much-quoted story of the sales seminar run by Mercuri Urval, the international business consultancy, where 30 higher-level managers were asked: 'What is your company's most important asset?' Their answers varied from 'Profit & Loss Account' to 'Buildings'; only one person said: 'the people'.

Business was invented by people, for people. Take away business, and there would still be people; but, take away people, and there would be no business. And business deals are struck when people get together in one way or another. At this stage, the only question you need to ask yourself is: *are you in business to stay in business, or are you in business just to make money?* How you answer this question will affect how you use this book.

The only problem with international business is that we are dealing with people from different cultures with different mind-sets from our own. Nonetheless, they are as eager to do business as we are – the difficulty lies in the fact that they will probably not want to do it in the way we're used to. This book is here to help, by providing the structures of different ways of thinking, using The Cultural Auras Theory (CAT), a new technique developed by Ron, interwoven with Neuro-Linguistic Programming (NLP) from Diana.

This combination will give you:

- the ability to analyse any situation you may find yourself in, depending on where you are
- a toolbox with the tools you will need to use, as a result of your analysis
- significantly improved chances of getting to YES!

So, where to begin? Let's start by thinking about a possible future scenario. Our product sells successfully at home, we're bored and stagnating, and we need a challenge. We've saturated the local market, and our spies tell us that our product would go down really well in a country that we know absolutely nothing about.

Before we even start to think about this new idea, the vital commodity we need is information.

The Map is not the Territory

We can get some of this information by looking at the atlas, and a map of the country. Maps are very informative, but they are only maps: two dimensional, very small and covered with symbols – and no one in their right minds would confuse them with the place itself.

Self-evident though this may seem, confusing the map with the territory is precisely what we are inclined to do. You have your model of the world inside your head, and we have our models; they're all different, and none of them is right or wrong: they are simply how we have all made sense of the information that we have about the world. Any policeman will tell you that, if you ask five witnesses to describe what happened, you will get five different versions of the event. Each person has adapted what they experienced to fit in with their model of the world; and each person is convinced that they are right, and that the others are wrong. As EM Forster would have it: 'the past is another country – they do things differently there.'

The more we expand our maps of the world by learning from other people's maps, the more we enrich our lives.

We can glean more information about this new country, from someone who's been there, from their Embassy, from the web, by talking to people who come from there, and by going there ourselves: local information is the key to our success – without it we can achieve nothing worthwhile. As we glean information from this far-flung country, our only cross-reference system is our own experience: we relate it to what we already know in order to make sense of it.

The same is true for marketing, sales, distribution, finance and any other aspect of international business. If we insist upon doing business our way, and imposing our map of the world upon these unfortunate people (and be assured, this happens a lot), it could be construed as telling them that they are doing everything 'wrong' – with the implication that they are idiots, out-of-date, small-minded, and so on. This may be the last thing we intend, but the overall result will be that we come across as superior, which makes them feel inferior; and would you want to do business with someone who made you feel inferior?

Fig 1.1 What do you see?

Looking at figure 1.1, do you see an old woman or a young woman? If you've seen this picture before, you'll know that it contains both women; if you haven't, you'll see one of them, and it may take you some time to see the other.

The young woman is looking away, over her left shoulder, and all you can see is her ear, her jawbone, her eyelashes and the tip of her nose. The old woman is mostly right profile, but turned more towards you, with her chin tucked down into her furs. The outline of the young woman's profile turns into the old woman's nose

The object of showing you this picture is to illustrate how people can come to completely different conclusions about what is 'right': imagine two people, one of whom can only see the old crone, and the other who can only see the young beauty. Each knows that he/she is right, and is convinced that the other is either an idiot or blind. This situation can happen all too often in business, when people are convinced that their way of doings things is 'the one right way'.

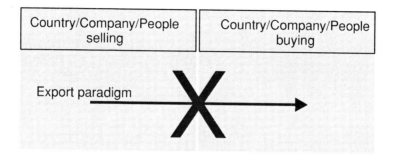

Fig 1.2a No Entry

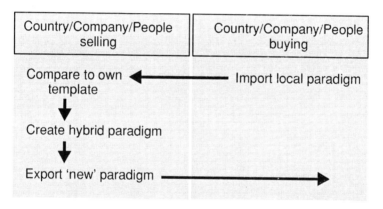

Fig 1.2 b: Two-way Traffic

Figure 1.2a shows the no-entry area: in other words, simply exporting our way of doing things probably won't work – other people like doing things their way as much as we do.

In figure 1.2b, we find the freeway for our business strategy. The trick is to study the local paradigms in the new area in which we wish to operate. Once we are satisfied about our understanding of, for instance, their local marketing, we can compare this to our own. We can then pool the resources of both sets of ideas, and produce a much more enriched and efficient map by way of a hybrid-marketing programme which contains the ingredients from both cultures and localities. This gives us something that we can relate to, and – more importantly – gives them something they can relate to and feel comfortable with.

Stirred, not Shaken

James Bond liked his martinis shaken, not stirred; but, if we shake up the company we want to do business with, we will certainly make them feel uncomfortable. The more likely result is that we will unnerve them completely about the prospect of doing business with us. However, if we gently stir the ingredients from both cultures together, we will produce a smooth amalgamation, which is palatable to both parties.

Before we launch into our new venture, there is a series of questions that we need to ask ourselves (these questions are discussed later on, in much more detail), for example:

1. Do we really understand this culture?
2. Do we also understand this particular culture's use of innuendo, whether it be in language, finance, the law, or rules (written or unwritten)?
3. Do we understand how relationships are created in this culture?
4. Do we know about their decision-making process, and how long it may take?
5. Do we know how these people might behave during, for instance, presentations?
6. Do we understand their model of how the world works?

If the answer to all these questions is 'yes' then any hurdles in our way will constitute no more than an exhilarating challenge.

Armed with this information, it might be interesting to go back to the times you haven't managed to get business for no apparent reason, and ask yourself the above questions about those projects. Doing this will give you some ideas about what you could have done differently, and how and where you could broaden your thinking.

1. Analyse the area/country we are about to visit.
2. Get some understanding of its history/culture.
3. Possibly learn some of the language.
4. Understand as much of their paradigms as possible.
5. Get some background information on the company.
6. Get some background information on its people.
7. Compare this information to your own environment.
8. Produce a paradigm which is acceptable to both.
9. Fine-tune the paradigm.
10. Be flexible.

10 steps for successful analysis

These are the 10 steps we need to take to increase our success abroad. As we do our research, we're looking for the differences from the way we do things at home, because it is the differences that will affect the way we set about our project.

1. Analyse the country/area we are about to visit*, and how its people think about business

For example, any presentation in the United Kingdom will start with the obligatory joke/s. This is essential (a) in order to keep the audience awake and listening, and (b) the audience needs to know that the presenter is human. In Germany, however, business is almost always conducted in a serious manner, so jokes might be considered as frivolous, in which case people won't take you seriously. It might, therefore, be unwise to think that the same presentation format will work in both countries.

To illustrate this, a very well-known NLP trainer went to Germany to run a workshop. By the end of the first day, the Germans were spitting with rage: *'the workshop had no structure. They were wasting their money.'* She sat up most of the night, rehashing her plans and the rest of the workshop went well. The next day, she flew to England to conduct the same workshop. She's spent so long revamping it that she gave them the new version (which had, after all, gone so well since the revamp). By the end of the first day, the

English were on strike: *'they hadn't spent all this money to be talked at. They wanted to **do** things.'*

Of course, there are Brits who do not like mixing humour with business, and there are Germans who like their business to be leavened with a flash of wit from time to time. So anything we say about any nation needs to be treated as a generalisation. As you will discover later on, it is the individual person within the overlay of his or her culture whom we are aiming to do business with.

2. Get some understanding of the history and culture*

For example, in the former Eastern Europe, people were suppressed for decades by the Communist regime. In those days, managers of manufacturing sites had no authority to discuss the prices of the raw materials they needed, because the Foreign Trade Office was in charge of buying everything from abroad. When the Wall came down, these unfortunate managers suddenly found themselves having to trade in these raw materials with little understanding of how this was done. Even now, these people are usually pretty sceptical when trading with the West – possibly because, in the early days, they lost out to more experienced western traders.

3. Learn at least some of the language

This may sound daunting – particularly if you are one of those English speakers who believe they are incapable of learning another language – but every word you utter demonstrates that you have put some effort into the visit, and are thus paying respect to their culture. The bonus is that a knowledge of the language give you a much greater insight into the culture itself. (There's a section on Lazy Language Learning in Chapter 9.)

4. Understand their paradigms

Have an awareness of how they are accustomed to doing business (you'll find much more about this in Chapter 3).

---

* Some useful sources of information – there are many more:
  - Governmental institutes (e.g. embassies, trade offices)
  - trade associations
  - the media
  - publications
  - authorities in the field.

5. Get some background information on the company

Now is the time to focus on the company or companies in question. We will need to analyse how they, as a company, do business. What is their corporate culture? What is different from what we are used to?

6. Get some background information on the people

The principle is the same as step 5, and we're now going down a level to try to get a picture of the people we are to deal with. How much external influence have they experienced? In other words, are they stuck in the middle of nowhere, or in a thriving international city? Are they accustomed to dealing with foreign companies? Are they accustomed to dealing with our country?

7. Compare this information to our own environment

It's now time to assemble our information, and compare it to what we take for granted when doing business at home. In this information, we're looking for sameness, and – more importantly – for difference: while the differences may create problems, we can use the sameness to create our hybrid.

8. Produce a paradigm which is acceptable to both parties

Once we are confident that we have enough information we can produce our hybrid paradigm: a way of working that will be acceptable to both parties.

9. Fine-tune the paradigm

Trial and error will show up any necessary fine-tuning, and over time, our strategy will become more refined and even more effective.

10. Be flexible!

The most flexible part of any system is the one which will survive the longest. When the hurricane comes, it is the solid trees that will blow down: the willows will bend with the wind, and survive. Flexibility will allow us to alter our plans to fit in with whatever comes up.

With this plan, and with clarity and persistence about achieving your goals, you will find the export world opening up to you.

To start you off, here is an exercise that will heighten your ability to notice the differences you will encounter when doing business in other countries. As you will see on page 27, we have drawn up a table of just some of the differences we need to be aware of. As you will realise, while we can usually adapt to environmental changes, our thoughts and behaviour are primarily based (for good or ill) upon our biology and the cultural influences of our upbringing.

Take this table with you, whenever you travel, and add your discoveries to it. This will sharpen your awareness, and increase your enjoyment of your exploration of cultural differences and their effects upon your less well-informed compatriots.

The trick is – insatiable curiosity. Open all your senses and notice what you notice.

Environment	Finance	Ancestry	Upbringing	Physical	Psychological
Climate Clothing Siestas Isolation from other cultures Winter darkness	Hedging Investment Payment terms Letters of credit	Genes Inheritance Tradition Physiology	Education Knowledge Intellect Religion Manners	Looks Health Dress Make-up	Self-esteem Compliance Sociability Humour Scepticism

The logical levels of thinking

Before we move on to CAT, we'd like to give you a useful overlay, which you can apply to any situation. The biologist and anthropologist, Gregory Bateson, arguably one of the great thinkers of our time, realised that we think at different logical levels, and this theory was further developed by Robert Dilts and the late Todd Epstein, of the NLP University in Santa Cruz, California.

In order to discover just how useful Logical Levels can be, let's use a simple school playground scenario. A has been nasty to B, and we have to sort out the situation.

Environment: Q. Where and when was A nasty to B?
A. In the playground at breaktime, after a maths lesson.

Behaviour: Q. What did he do?
A. He knocked him over

Capability: Q. How did he do it?
A. He charged at him

Beliefs/values: Q. Why did he do it?
A. He hates maths, the lesson went badly, and B had told him he was stupid – like the rest of his family.

Identity: Q. Who is A in this situation?
A. A big boy, with low self-esteem who's lost his cool.

Who else?   Q. In this scene, who is A in relation to others?
A. Someone who's not prepared to have his family insulted.

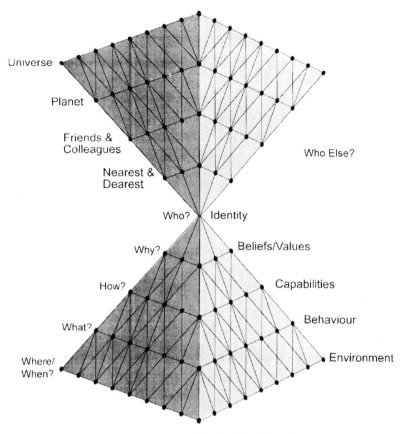

Developed by Robert Dilts and the late Todd Epstein
This version © Diana Beaver

Fig 1.3 – Gregory Bateson's Logical Levels of Thinking

If we start at the top of figure 1.3, as we look down, we see that each level is a part of the system above it: the planet is part of the universe; our friends, colleagues, associates, are a part of the planet; our nearest and dearest form a part of our friends; we form a part of the system that makes up our nearest and dearest; our beliefs and values are a part of who we are; our capabilities are acquired because of our beliefs and values and so on.

By the same token, we can see that everything filters downwards: who we are in relation to our nearest and dearest affects who we are as people;

29

who we are as people affects our beliefs and values; our beliefs and values affect our capabilities: if we believe we can't do maths, we won't be able to do it – or if we believe that learning another language is worthless, we won't do it; and our capabilities affect our behaviour.

As you will see, beliefs and values (which come from our culture) are very high-level, just below who we are. We mess with other people's beliefs and values at our peril, because their beliefs and values are the basis for who they are. Likewise, if we are rude about their family or their country, or their company, we could find ourselves in trouble, because those are something they belong to: this is part of who they are in connection to the wider world.

It is interesting to eavesdrop on people who have hardly been abroad (or people one would expect to know better) when they travel in a new country for the first time. They have, quite properly, been brought up to believe that their nation is the greatest in the world; and, when they see these poor, benighted foreigners doing things differently (i.e. 'wrongly', according to their upbringing), you may hear gales of laughter, or shocked disbelief at the backwardness, or scandalised comments on the disgrace of it all.

Probably the most useful thing about Logical Levels is that it makes quite clear that what other people do is just 'behaviour' and it makes no difference to who they are.

People are individuals and it is people who are responsible for doing business. It is not the company that does business, nor the Profit/Loss account, nor some tangible asset (although these factors will affect decisions), it is purely and simply the individuals. And this is why we need to analyse how business people think in different countries, in order to create the relationship in which we can do business effectively.

Life and Mind are Systemic Processes

NL-People think in terms of systems, which is why we have brought in Logical Levels at this stage. Our company is a system; the company we hope to do business with is a system; our relationship with our opposite number in the other company is a system. And the thing about any system in which we are playing a part is that everything we do affects that system in one way or another. Some examples: if we are having a conversation with another person, everything that we say and do is going to affect that person's response to us; or, if we dam a river, to help the farmers upstream, it is also going to affect the farmers downstream; or, if we pass new laws to protect some people, these new laws may adversely affect other people, and so on. Everything changes all the time, and it's the process of change that we are going to think about.

At this point, and before we move on to the Cultural Auras Theory, we want to remind you again that everything we say about different cultures is a sweeping generalisation. Each individual has a different mind-set within the parameters of his or her culture. For example, the Dutch have a reputation for being good traders. The reasoning behind this is that Dutch were obliged to trade, as they had little or no natural resources of their own except for some farming land and a huge amount of water. They were very good at trade: the Dutch East India Company had the monopoly of trade with the Far East for the best part of 200 years. Also, anti-semitism in Holland meant that the only thing the Jews were allowed to trade in was what St Paul called 'filthy lucre', so many of the great banking houses were established by Jews. But, for every good Dutch trader, you'll find as many hopeless ones.

Further afield, you'll find Iranians who have spent several years living in the USA and have returned to Iran to set up their own businesses; you will also find Iranians who have never set foot outside the town or village they were born in. And, while only 10% of US citizens have passports, of that 10% there are many who are widely travelled and speak several languages.

These examples serve as a reminder that we need to treat generalisations as important influences, which create underlying cultural undertones, but they do not – nor ever could – describe individuals.

Back to our research: any general worth his salt will research his enemy thoroughly, to discover not only what equipment he has and what his capabilities are, but also – as far as possible – what goes on in his head: how he will respond to given situations. And, while we are hoping that the people we plan to work with will become friends, the army maxim that 'time spent in reconnaissance is never wasted' also holds true for business.

Before we move on to thinking about building relationships with people of other cultures, here is a summary of this chapter.

Success Checklist

1. If what you're doing now isn't working, it's time to do something different.

2. Business is about people.

3. Different cultures think differently and do things differently.

4. Information is our most important commodity.

5. Create a hybrid paradigm to suit both cultures.

6. How people behave, and what they believe, has nothing to do with who they are.

7. The map is not the territory, and generalisations are not facts.

8. Everything that we do affects the system we are in at the time.

9. Time spent in reconnaissance is never wasted.

2

The Cultural Auras Theory – A New Toolbox for International Business

As we saw earlier, people buy people, and business is above all about relationships. Ron has developed his Cultural Auras Theory to put a simple, recognisable structure on what happens – stage by stage – when people from different cultures get together to create a relationship, whether it be business or social.

In some cultures, the major difference between business and social relationships is the length of time it takes before we are allowed, or allow others, a greater degree of closeness. In other cultures, business and social relationships are barely distinguishable and even interrelated.

The basis of the theory

The theory is based on the four phases of a relationship, and can be used as a tool to improve or establish relationships both at work and at play. Each of these phases is sub-divided into four sub-phases as we will show later. These phases are based upon the distance (physical or metaphorical) that we maintain between ourselves and other people in the course of conversation.

E T Hall (see bibliography) posited that we have four zones of personal distance:

Zone	Distance	Situation
1. Public	3.5m – 7.5m (11'8" – 25')	Meetings and ceremonies Speakers/audiences
2. Social	1.2m – 3.5m (4' – 11'8")	Business conversations, Discussions with strangers
3. Personal	0.45m – 1.2m (1'6" – 4')	Friends, Family members
4. Intimate	0 – 0.45m (0 – 1'6")	Lovers, Very close family (e.g.. mother and child), Very close friends

Zones of Personal Distance

1. The **Public Zone** relates to the distance, say, between speakers and their audiences, or between the organisers and the rest, at public meetings or ceremonies. The formality of this zone decrees a greater degree of separation.
2. The **Social Zone** covers situations like business conversations, and discussions between acquaintances or strangers. These are more interactive, and therefore require more closeness to achieve their purpose.
3. The **Personal Zone** is, of its essence, 'close': among friends and family. Therefore the space is reduced even more.
4. The **Intimate Zone** is reserved for lovers, close family members (think of a mother and child), and our closest of close friends.

These distances will also vary between cultures, for example, between the north and south of Europe. Northern Europeans may well find themselves overcrowded by the closeness required by Southern Europeans – while people with southern warmth may find the colder northerners 'stand-offish'.

Do you ever find yourself having to move away from someone who is talking to you, in order to give yourself more space; or, alternatively, do you find that people you are talking to you move back, away from you? This happens when you and your interlocutor have different ideas about safe space: about the space we need around us in order to feel comfortable and to function properly. There's no one right space. All we need is the awareness that other people's needs may be different, plus the flexibility to fit in with them, and give them the closeness or the distance that they require.

After over 20 years of experience, it became apparent to Ron that there were four main stages in a business relationship. He has christened them 'auras' because they surround us, they are flexible, they vary in size and they have hazy boundaries.

- The **Formal Business Aura** surrounds and protects each individual at the first encounter between two or more business people. It's a straight defence mechanism: we are far enough away to notice any movement that might threaten danger, and respond accordingly, with fight or flight.

- The **Friendly Business Aura** covers the next stage, as the friendliness increases, and the formality relaxes. This person seems safe enough, we can move a bit closer.

- **Friendly Personal Aura** is available at the third stage, as we get to know and trust the other individual/s better. We have tested this person out, and believe we have nothing to fear, so we can let our barriers down. Here the conversation may become more personal, as a result of the developing relationship.

- The **Inner Core** is available only to people who are very close; and it is rare to reach this level in business.

These four auras are divided into two distinctive groups: the outer self and the inner self. These two are not separated by strict boundaries, but flow into one another.

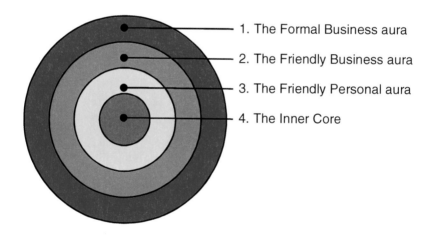

1. The Formal Business aura
2. The Friendly Business aura
3. The Friendly Personal aura
4. The Inner Core

Figure 2.1 – The Cultural Auras

As you will see from fig 2.1, moving inwards from the outside, the outer-self (the outer two circles) contains the Formal Business Aura and the Friendly Business Aura, while the inner-self (the inner two circles) contains the Friendly Personal Aura and the Inner Core. This last is rarely opened up, other than partially to a spouse or a very good friend.

Auras 1 and 2 may intertwine because, in some cultures, the Formal Business Aura hardly exists, and we will often find ourselves moving straight into Friendly Business.

In other cultures, we won't be invited into Friendly Business until a certain degree of trust has been established, but here we will find that Friendly Business and Friendly Personal may overlap. In other words, once there is trust, we may find ourselves passing very quickly into Friendly Personal.

Auras, of course, have colour and hazy boundaries; but, for simplicity, we've used black, grey, silver and white – to make it easier for you to imagine how the sizes differ, and how they can merge into each other.

E T Hall	C A T	
Public	Formal business	The outer-self
Social	Friendly business	
Personal	Friendly personal	The inner-self
Intimate	Inner core	

Comparison of the Cultural Auras to Hall's Zones

While CAT and Hall do not exactly correspond (for example, there is a huge difference in size between the Public Zone and the Formal Business Aura), they are still worth the comparison.

As well changing our personal space, we also change our language according to the aura we may find ourselves in. Let's imagine a possible conversation after a classical concert, depending on the relationship we have with our companion/s.

1. Formal Business	It was excellent. I enjoyed it very much.
2. Friendly Business	It was marvellous. I'm so glad we came.
3. Friendly Personal	That was so evocative! I used to come to concerts here with my first girlfriend.
4. Inner-Core	You know, I played that last piece over and over again when my mother died, and it helped me to cope

Language variations according to aura

Each comment shows appreciation of the concert: the first is completely formal; the second adds the acknowledgement of the pleasure of other person/people's company; the third reveals a personal memory; while the fourth offers personal information that probably hasn't been shared with many people.

In business too, we will come across differing responses at the different levels – not only in the space people maintain around them and what they say, but in their facial expressions, eye contact, intonation, physiology, stress level and so on. As always, these parameters are influenced by culture and we shall discuss these influences in much greater depth later on.

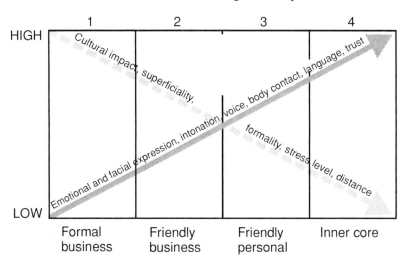

Fig 2.2 – Observable changes from aura to aura

Figure 2.2 shows the changes we experience as we move through the Auras. We have two different sets of priorities to think about: one starts in the bottom left hand corner, and the other starts in the top left.

Top left – at our first business meeting, we may be nervous – or stressed after a long journey. We may withdraw into ourselves, into the safety of what we know, our culture – where we'll keep our distance, with formal language and superficial conversation. What we know, and what will keep us safe, both have a high priority.

Bottom left – our real self stays down in the bottom left hand corner. We keep our gestures controlled, we maintain a neutral tone of voice and a reasonably impassive expression on our face. We believe that, if we reveal too much of ourselves, it might be inappropriate at this juncture. If both sides are behaving in this way, the discussion may well be stiff and unproductive.

Over time, as we are allowed into the Friendly Business Aura and the Friendly Personal Aura, these priorities will shift. Conversation becomes more relaxed and lively as, gradually, we start to show more emotion in our face, our tone of voice, and our gestures. As trust is established, there will be more eye contact, and more closeness, both mental and physical. And, as this happens, the importance of our cultural safety net, and all that goes with it, will diminish.

The definitions of the auras

We are now going to go into the auras in more detail.

Auras	Definitions
1. Formal Business	The level for the first meeting. Usually formal and very neutral in attitude.
2. Friendly Business	The level for the established beginning of a relationship.
3. Friendly Personal	The level for a sound trusting relationship
4. Inner-Core	The level for a relationship of deep trust and intimacy (rarely reached in business)

The Cultural Auras and where to expect to find yourself

This table illustrates what aura you can expect to find yourself in, according to the development of a particular business relationship.

1. The Formal Business Aura

As we saw above, when two people meet for the first time, their language, attitude, sense of humour and overall behaviour will, in general, be calm and serious. They will keep their distance, there will be little eye contact, no physical contact – except for a hand-shake, and little facial and emotional expression. This is the non-committal aura – we're not ready to commit ourselves either to business or to the relationship.

Because of cultural influences, the length of time spent in Formal Business may well be greater in Asia, Japan, and Western and Central Europe than, for instance, in the USA. The language will be formal in most European, Asian and Middle Eastern countries, and people will address one another by title and surname or Sir or Madam. In the UK, people will probably address one another by their first names, as in the USA, though it is essential to note here that there is far more formality in the UK than there is in the US.

In some cultures, a level of formality may even be maintained in Friendly Personal, and sometimes in Inner Core: for example, in Germany, long-term acquaintances may still address one another as Herr Doktor; and, in France, some married couples may call each other '*vous*', which is considered to be more respectful than the informal '*tu*'.

Incidentally, in France, the concept of addressing someone as '*tu*' is a minefield; so we need to address everyone (except small children) as '*vous*' until asked to do otherwise. '*Tu*' can paradoxically imply both personal closeness and also disrespect. For example, when a policemen addresses a suspect as '*tu*', the suspect is well within his or her rights to demand more respect. One of the greatest put-downs in France, coming in response to the suggestion: '*on se tutoye?*' (meaning: 'shall we call each other '*tu*' from now on, instead of '*vous*'?'), is '*si vous voulez*' ('if you want to' – using the formal you). Also we need to address every man as '*monsieur*' and every woman as '*madame*' or '*mademoiselle*' until asked to do otherwise – it's all to do with showing respect, which is the most important thing we can do for anybody. In some French families, the parents will address a child as '*tu*', but will expect the children to call them '*vous*', out of respect for their elders.

And the same goes for first names. When Mr John Smith meets Monsieur Henri Dupont for the first time and addresses him as 'Henri', the immediate, and offended, response may well be: 'Mr. Smith, shall we stick to 'Mr. Dupont'?'

In the Middle East, colleagues will address one another by their title, and, even if your friend Reza and the well-respected Dr Mehdi Mirsalimi are on first name terms, Reza will tell you: 'Doctor Mirsalimi agrees with your proposal', if you and the good Doctor are not on first name terms. While this may seem perfectly normal to Europeans, it can flummox visitors from the US who expect him to refer to his friend as Mehdi.

In German, (unless they've reached the Inner Core) people may still address each other as '*Sie*' (formal 'you'), although it means 'they' when it hasn't got a capital letter (you can only tell the difference when it's written down, which causes confusion).

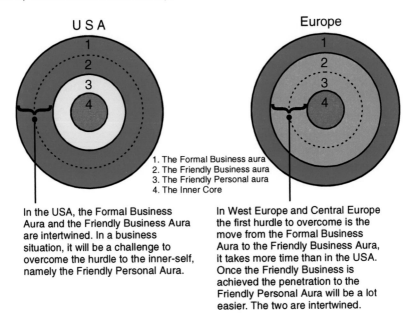

USA

Europe

1. The Formal Business aura
2. The Friendly Business aura
3. The Friendly Personal aura
4. The Inner Core

In the USA, the Formal Business Aura and the Friendly Business Aura are intertwined. In a business situation, it will be a challenge to overcome the hurdle to the inner-self, namely the Friendly Personal Aura.

In West Europe and Central Europe the first hurdle to overcome is the move from the Formal Business Aura to the Friendly Business Aura, it takes more time than in the USA. Once the Friendly Business is achieved the penetration to the Friendly Personal Aura will be a lot easier. The two are intertwined.

Fig 2.3 – CAT in Europe compared to the USA

Figure 2.3 compares CAT in Europe and the US. As you will see, in the US, Formal and Friendly Business are the same blue, because there is not much difference between them; whereas, in Europe, Friendly Business and Friendly Personal are similarly blended, because there is not much difference between them (see 'Friendly Business' below). You may find that, in most countries, it takes a lot of time and effort to move from the first to the second aura, both socially and in business, whereas in the US (especially in the West and South) this can happen very quickly. Although the move may take somewhat longer in the East and North of the USA, these two auras are very much intertwined in comparison with the countries we mentioned above.

An alternative and graphic way of seeing this idea is shown below, where progress is from left to right. The overlapping auras are clearly shown and the differences between the US approach and the European one are obvious.

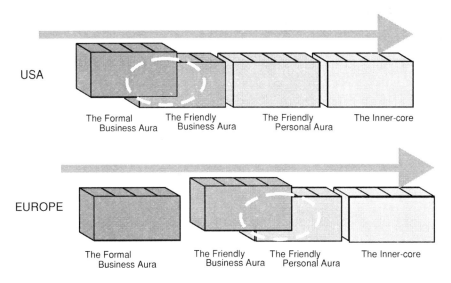

Figure 2.4 – CAT in Europe compared to the USA (model 2)

We shall use this left-to-right imagery again to describe the changing patterns of aura as found in different circumstances and locations.

2. The Friendly Business Aura

We may find ourselves included in this aura at a first meeting, or it may take years, once again depending on the culture. In this aura we discover that the language used is less formal, there is room for humour, the physiology will change, and people will be more relaxed, when the trust between the parties has increased.

Once again, the speed at which we reach Friendly Business, and move into Friendly Personal will depend upon the culture. In Japan, on the whole, this process takes a long time; but it will be greatly reduced if one takes the trouble to learn Japanese, and to understand this very exciting culture better.

Timings differ in the USA from South to North, and from East to West – but on the whole, the first and second auras are intertwined. That is to say that, in the USA, we will spend only a fraction of the time in the first aura in contrast to Europe. It is also worth noting here that, in the Mid-West of the USA, primarily the centre of the country, it will take longer to get to from Friendly Business to Friendly Personal than, for instance, in most parts of Europe, where Auras 2 and 3 are very much intertwined.

Once we have been invited into Friendly Business in, say, Belgium or Italy, Friendly Personal is easily accessible, and this allows people to discuss any personal problems that might affect their meeting. In France, M Dupont may become Henri; in Italy you may get a friendly pat and, throughout Europe, irrelevant family matters may be discussed during business meetings. In the Former East European and Middle Eastern countries, including Russia, you might get a kiss on both cheeks (and this includes men), and, in the USA, you might be invited home for dinner.

3. The Friendly Personal Aura

While the barrier between Formal Business and Friendly Business may take an effort to overcome in some cultures; it may take more effort to move from Friendly Business to Friendly Personal in others. A lot of business, especially long-term, is done in this aura. Once the relationship has been established, there is free movement between Friendly Business and Friendly Personal. The trust factor is critical, body language will have changed significantly, people may touch each other frequently – depending on the culture; the intonation of the voice will have changed dramatically compared to Formal Business; people will show more emotion and their faces will be much more expressive; the distance between them will have reduced, and the overall attitude will be one of commitment. In this aura, business matters are discussed in a very relaxed way (see table above The Cultural Auras and where to expect to find yourself). This is the most productive aura, and is the one we need to aim for when discussing business.

As we have seen, in some parts of the USA, it is easy to get access to the Friendly Business Aura as it is intertwined with Formal Business. Americans are very friendly, and may well reveal more of their outer selves than the average European; but, with them, Friendly Personal may be less accessible. In Europe, the outer and inner self are intertwined; whereas this is where the main barrier will be found in the central parts of the USA.

In the USA, business commitments are often made at the first meeting, because 'time is money'. Usually, the deals are sealed by lawyers, who may even be present at the meeting. However, in most other areas, people need to build up a relationship, in order to ensure that their goals are achieved by mutual trust – rather than by lawyers.

Because the Americans take time to reveal their inner selves, Europeans may think of them as superficial; Americans, on the other hand may regard Europeans as reserved because, at the outset, they present only their Formal Business Aura.

While, in Friendly Personal, people will reveal a fair amount of their inner selves, and possibly some emotional issues, Herr Doktor may, nonetheless, remain Herr Doktor in Germany.

4. The Inner Core Aura

In business, this is the least essential and, as we saw earlier, only accessible to good friends and spouses. While it may be the least essential, it is also the most powerful. Ron does business with people who have become close friends, and they will discuss things with him that they would never reveal to their spouses. At this level, there is no need to haggle about prices, as the trust between them is total.

The two diagrams below show some of the differences that you will find in the auras throughout the world, which we shall discuss in more detail in subsequent chapters.

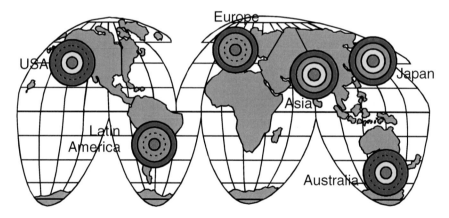

In North America as well as in Australia, it is easier to go from the Formal Business aura to the Friendly Business aura than in the other parts of the world. Due to this phenomenon, business can be conducted more readily in these former areas.
It will take more time to achieve similar results in Latin America, Europe and Asia - especially Japan. In the latter areas, it is essential to establish a relationship and to go to at least the Friendly Business aura to obtain these results.
   The overlap of the *Formal Business* and *Friendly Business* auras are similar in North America and Australia, whereas in the other parts of the world the overlaps of the *Friendly Business* aura and the *Friendly Personal* aura are similar to show the easy overflow in the different parts.

Fig 2.4 – CAT in different areas around the world

Looking at Figure 2.4, you will notice that the Formal and Friendly Business Auras in the USA and Australia look much the same: in both countries, the shift from Formal to Friendly Business happens with ease. Whereas, in the other parts of the world, the first shift takes longer; but, once made, the move from Friendly Business to Friendly Personal is almost automatic.

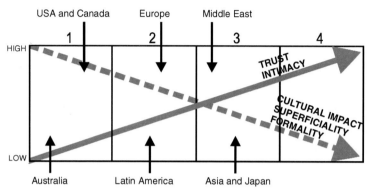

In the USA and Australia it is less essential to build a relationship than in Europe, Latin America or Asia and Japan. Business in the USA can be readily conducted in the first aura (1) whereas in the other areas it is in the Friendly Business aura. This is primarily because business is solidified by lawyers much more in the USA than in the other parts of the world. Note that in Asia – Japan it is closer to the third aura than in Latin America and/or Europe in general. It is essential to build a trust in Europe, Latin America and Asia – Japan as business is conducted in a trust-related fashion and not necessarily by the blessing of lawyers.

Fig 2.5 – The importance of trust building for most of the world areas

In Figure 2.5 we see that, in the USA as well as in Australia, we can do business in the first aura: the line starting in the bottom left hand corner shows the importance of the relationship, and the line starting in the top left shows the importance of lawyers. We need to be in Friendly Business in Europe and Latin America, while in the Middle East, Asia and Japan, we need to be in Friendly Personal. And you will also notice that, in the Middle East, Asia and Japan, lawyers are of little or no importance – here the handshake is more important, as it would be utterly disgraceful to renegue on a deal over which one has shaken hands. And, if we were doing business in the Inner Core, the idea of lawyers would be quite ridiculous.

Identifying the aura we find ourselves in during our business encounters

On the whole, people demonstrate an up-beat mode in Formal and Friendly Business. They affect good humour. They will not reveal problems in Formal Business, and they will minimise them in Friendly Business, for example 'We're struggling these days – but we'll survive.'

Once we reach the Friendly Personal Aura, we may get very different information, for instance: 'I am actually frightened of what is going to happen if this trend continues', or 'It's going very well, but I wonder whether we can maintain this trend?'

Here are some examples of what we might discuss in the different auras.

1. Formal Business	Introduction of the people, the company, the products. General and superficial information.
2. Friendly Business	Products and business are discussed in greater detail. Some aspects of personal information may be exchanged. Short-term business may be concluded.
3. Friendly Personal	Very personal information may be exchanged as a consequence of growing trust. Business, especially long-term, is usually concluded in this aura.
4. Inner-Core	In many cultures, long-term business is maintained in this aura. (Note: it floats between Friendly Personal and Inner-Core.) The business itself is discussed on a need-to-know basis. Intimate, more personal, information may also be discussed. (E.g. the impact of depression, divorce, death of a relative etc)

Discussions appropriate for the different auras

1. In the reserved, exploratory **Formal Business Aura**, we would expect simply to introduce our company and its products or services, and exchange general, superficial information with the other party. We go with the flow, if this is a culture we're not used to, and let the other party make the running.
2. As we saw above, time is money in the USA, so contrary to this summary, we might well find ourselves in **Friendly Business** more or less straight away, and even concluding short-term business. But, in the

rest of the world, business people are not generally accompanied by phalanxes of lawyers at this stage (if at all); so, if no one is ready to do business with us yet, we still need to go with the flow and discuss our company and products in greater detail. If we feel it is appropriate, we can exchange some small snippets of personal information here.

3. **Friendly Personal** is the place to be! Here we can exchange much more personal information; for example, anxiety about the future, the birth of a child, our spouse, what our children are up to, the acquisition of a company (which is not yet common knowledge), and ways of helping each other's businesses. This is where the trust is; this is where we find the space to conclude long-term business.

4. The **Inner Core** is an even better place to be; and, in many cultures this is where long-term business is maintained – although it can also happen in Friendly Personal. Here business is discussed on a need-to-know basis; there is no haggling over prices, as trust is complete; and, here, more intimate personal issues can be discussed, such as depression, divorce, a death in the family.

How do we do all this?

So, all we need to do is to get into someone's Friendly Personal Aura, or Inner Core, and the business will be ours. The only question left is 'How do we do that?'

It's a simple fact of life that we 'like' people who are 'like' ourselves. Teenagers will adopt the clothes, behaviour, language and hairstyles of the group they want to be accepted by; football supporters buy the strip and learn the songs; IT consultants have their own dress-down uniform, with the latest 'in' sunglasses, plus the smallest mobile telephones on the market; businessmen wear suits, and so it goes on. As St Ambrose advised St Augustine in the 4th century: 'When you are in Rome, live in Roman style; when you are elsewhere, live as they live elsewhere.'

The trick, when one finds oneself in another culture, is to be a chameleon: to change behaviour to fit in with the social mores of the country we are in, so that we don't stand out, and no one will be embarrassed by us. In India, for example, shorts and T-shirts are considered as underwear; so, for a visiting woman who wants to be cool and comfortable but can't cope with a sari, the most comfortable thing to wear is Punjabi dress, so that all offending limbs are covered. We can fly out early in trousers, or a long skirt, with a long-sleeved top, and kit ourselves out there – clothes are incredibly cheap in India.

Making the effort demonstrates courtesy and respect, which may come as a great surprise to business people who are not used to foreigners making an effort; and this will stand you in good stead in the long term.

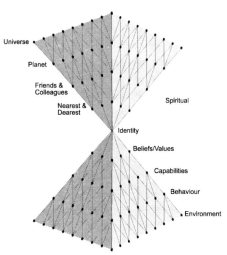

Here is the 'logical levels' diagram again – to save your having to search for it.

By fitting in with another culture, you could be excused for thinking that you have just changed your behaviour, and that it's hardly worth the effort; but the result of that change is going to affect your colleague at a much higher level. You are, at an unconscious level, honouring his/her culture, something that he/she belongs to; and this is way above identity level, and very powerful magic – particularly when your colleague compares you to your competitors who didn't bother, and thereby showed disrespect for the culture – with the result that nobody wanted to give them the business.

Here's an exercise for you to do before you go off on your next trip abroad

Spend some time 'manwatching', to borrow the title of Desmond Morris's fascinating book (see bibliography). Take some time for yourself, settle yourself down with a refreshing drink and watch people who are spending time together. You'll notice that friends walk in step with each other, stride for stride; that they sit in the same way as each other; that they nod in unison; that they make the same gestures: their minds and their bodies are in tune.

Then you can spend time doing with this with people you would like to get to know better - and see what happens.

When you arrive at your next foreign destination, you can take some time out before your first appointment and repeat the exercise in this different culture and notice what you notice. What are the differences between the way friends and strangers treat each other here from the way they do back home? Equipped with your new information, you can create a solid rapport with your new colleague. Let's assume, for simplicity, that he's a man.

All you need to do is simply copy his physiology: walk in step with him, sit the same way that he is sitting, smile when he smiles, frown when he frowns, drink when he drinks and breathe when he breathes (this last is easier than you might think: if he's talking, breathe in when he stops for breath). By aligning your physiology, you will be aligning your minds, and you'll be astounded at how well you find yourselves getting on.

The only problem with NLP is that it is too simple, so people assume that it can't possibly work. So, as Steve Andreas, the world-renowned NLP trainer and author would say: 'You owe it to your scepticism to try this out'.

Opening up our own Friendly Personal Aura

The fastest, simplest and most effective way of creating rapport with another person, is to look deep into his/her right eye and pretend 'this person really matters to me'. The other stuff is behaviour-level; this is identity-level, and consequently even more powerful. Diana had a client who didn't have any friends at school; she gave her this task for a week and, by the end of the week, she had a whole mass of friends, and they really did matter to her. But there is a caveat: in some cultures, eye contact is considered disrespectful: do your homework!

Behaviour-level rapport is one thing, and could be construed as manipulative; identity-level rapport is quite another – think about your nearest and dearest: they may do things that drive you mad, but you still love them for who they are. As we have said all the way along – it's the person that matters, so let's walk our talk by dealing with them at identity level and above.

Success Checklist

1. Different situations require different 'safe distances'.

2. Different cultures maintain different distances.

3. Different auras require different behaviours.

4. The Friendly Personal Aura is where we want to be.

5. We 'like' people who are 'like' us.

6. Respect and honour the other culture.

7. Spend time manwatching.

8. Behave like the other person/people in the new culture.

9. Remember - 'This person really matters to me.'

3

First Impressions – Sub-auras Part I: Physical and Behavioural

The Sub-Auras

Each of the four auras we have discussed can be further subdivided into four sub-auras (see Figure 3.1); working from the outside in, they are: the physical, the behavioural, the technical and the mental, and these are based on what we observe, and what we subsequently discover about the other person.

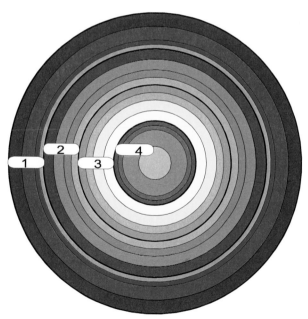

Fig 3.1a – The four sub-auras within each aura

These sub-auras are integral to the main ones. You will notice that their sizes vary significantly according to the way we view and/or approach people, and the impact of their cultural backgrounds upon us. The physical and behavioural aspects are much more important in the business auras, whereas the technical and mental have more impact in the personal auras.

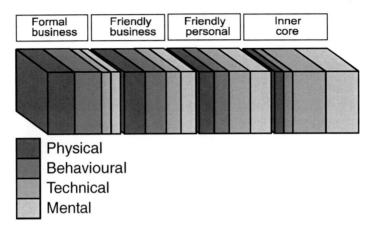

Fig 3.1b – The sub-auras

The breakdown in Figure 3.1b shows how the importance of the different sub auras reverse themselves as we move from left to right, from the outside (Formal Business) in to the Inner Core. In Formal Business, at our first meeting, what people look like, and how they behave, are going to influence our first impressions greatly: in this aura, we are going to pay little attention to the technical and mental side. Whereas, at the other end of the scale, once we are in the Inner Core, the technical and mental aspects are what matter, and we pay virtually no attention to appearances and behaviour.

1. The physical sub-aura

First impressions

There's an expression in the design world that goes something like: 'the first bite is visual', which nicely combines the concept of 'taste' and what things look like.

Opinion is divided about how much time we've got, to make that all-important first impression, but it's probably about three seconds; and the physical sub-aura is all about what we look like, what we sound like, and what can be immediately perceived about us in general. If any of this does not correspond to the other person's culture (or with what they have learned to expect as normal from *our* culture), it will be recorded at a conscious or unconscious level and may be interpreted as lack of respect, or bad manners or something completely different. So, a woman going to a business meeting in India wearing a short skirt and a sleeveless blouse would be a cultural disaster: her hosts would respond in the way that we would respond if someone came to a business meeting with us in their underwear. They would probably be quite charming, but they would never forget the shock.

Most people respond to visual input – hence the popularity of television and computer screens; for example, how many people have told you: 'I forget names, but I never forget a face'? So, when they meet someone for the first time, their eyes take in the information, and compare and contrast it with the information in their visual databanks. If what they see does not fit in with their images of the sort of person they like to associate with, and if they haven't read this book, we might hear things like ...

> 'Where *did* he find that suit?'
> 'Have you seen her hair?'
> 'He looks as though he's come straight out of the jungle!'
> 'She's blonde – she must be a bimbo.'

... or other instant judgements, devoid of conscious thought – none of which is conducive to building a relationship of trust. And, while we may regard this as utterly superficial, nonetheless, the barrier is up.

Matters of dress

What people look like generally incorporates what they are wearing. As you will see from figure 3.2, people's choice of clothes is often driven by the culture they come from.

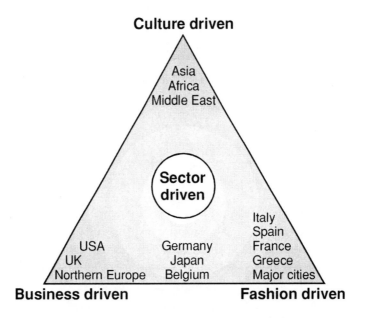

Fig 3.2 – Some different dress codes, and how they have evolved.

Business driven: This is what we're used to! In the UK, Northern Europe and most of the US, we wear suits with or without ties – depending on gender. Functional, not flashy – we wouldn't want to draw attention to ourselves, after all.

Culture driven (and, here culture can include religion): Indian and Iranian men, for example, will be buttoned up to the neck, but without ties; in Islamic cultures, women may be covered from head to toe. In the African countries, some Asian countries and in the Middle East we will find traditional/local dress codes, which we may not be accustomed too. But, in major cities around the world, this may be different.

Fashion driven: Mediterranean people are pretty clothes conscious so, in Italy, Spain, France, Greece, it is important for business clothes to be fashionable: this can range from a Paul Shark sweater to an Armani suit for the men, and the women are definitely chic and more daring in their dress (for example, a woman may show more leg in Italy than you'll see in the USA). We'll also find fashion driven business dress in major cities around the world.

Sector driven: it is now 'in' to dress down in the computer world, and be gadget- instead of clothes-orientated. The smallest and latest mobile phones (cell phones) and the right kind of sunglasses are more important than clothes.

The old school, working in the City of London (the financial sector), can still be seen in their pin-striped suits with their rolled umbrellas, but the young may be more into Armani.

Business and fashion combined: the Germans, Belgians and Japanese like a more chic version of conventional business wear: their clothes have more chic than in Northern Europe, but are more restrained than in Southern Europe.

2. The behavioural sub-aura

After they have scanned us for what we look like, the next thing people will probably notice is our behaviour: the way we talk, the way we move, our manners, our gestures and so on. And all this too will be influenced by the culture they come from: harmless gestures in one culture can be the height of rudeness in another (see Desmond Morris's *Gestures* in the bibliography). The observers will search their cultural databanks for something with which to compare and contrast this new information. If nothing sensible is available, they may come up with responses like:

'Typical Jewish/black/Indian/Arab!'
'What appalling manners!' (maybe someone from the Middle East is eating with his fingers).

What we hear and don't hear

People will also be listening, and may enchanted by, or take against, a tone of voice, a choice of words, an accent: the English are much more auditory than the Americans, and can quickly respond unfavourably to a tonality they don't like. There is also the cultural difference between straight talking and circumlocution, which we shall discuss later in this chapter.

The language within the language

While language as such can be pretty slippery, and contributes only about 7% of what we really mean, it's the nearest we can get to exactitude in, for example, a letter. We consider language to be so important that we have devoted a whole chapter to it later on.

Figure 3.3 below explains the different levels of formality in language that we use in our communication with one another (the technical term is 'Register'). For example, imagine that the Bishop has been invited to Sunday lunch, the sauce is going round and, depending on who is offering it to whom, the words will be different.

Waitress to Bishop: 'Would you like some sauce, Your Grace?'
Hostess to Bishop: 'Can I pass you some sauce, Bishop?'
Father to Son: 'Sauce?'
Brother to Sister: 'Want some sauce?'

The waitress is there as staff, so she gives the Bishop his official form of address; the hostess knows the Bishop reasonably well; Father doesn't need any extra words and the brother, without his father's sophistication, and having shifted from 'would you like?' to 'do you want?' doesn't deem it necessary to use all the words. In the UK, offering something by saying 'do you want' is, paradoxically, either rude and uncaring, or a covert admission that you are almost family.

Oliver Goldsmith's *She Stoops to Conquer* (1775) has its comedy based almost entirely on register. Our hero arrives to visit the young lady whom his father has decided he shall marry. He puts up at what he is told is an inn but which is, in fact the house of his intended. He talks to his prospective father-in-law as he would to an innkeeper; while his father-in-law talks to him as though he were an honoured guest. Our hero's main problem is that he is desperately shy in polite society so, when he meets his intended for the first time, he cannot bring himself even to look at her – let alone woo her with sweet nothings; however, he gets on capitally with barmaids and serving wenches. Once our heroine is made aware of this, she pretends to be a serving wench; he is instantly smitten, they get on famously conversing in completely informal (if not vulgar) language, and live happily ever after.

British English is full of implication and circumlocution, and can be a minefield for the unwary. As you will see from figure 3.3, other nations give it to you straight: what you hear is what you get. The left and right hand quadrants relate to the formality or informality of language used, while the top and bottom quadrants relate to circumlocution or straight talking.

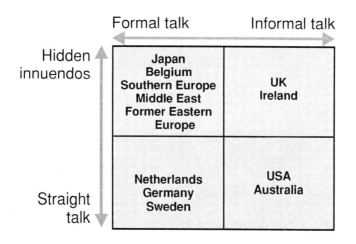

Fig 3.3 – Talking the talk

In the top left quadrant, where the language is formal and vague, we find the Japanese, the Belgians, the Southern Europeans, the former Eastern Europeans and the countries of the Middle East. At our first meeting, we can expect great formality, and this may last for some time. These cultures are famous for talking in metaphor and leaving things unsaid, but expecting you to understand what they mean. They want to send the signal that they are not yet ready to be pinned down – but, of course, they couldn't possibly say that.

To illustrate this point, Ron was giving a presentation to a group of Americans from the Mid-West and some Japanese, on strategies for business and product development: the Americans interrupted, and asked some tough questions, while the Japanese just listened and postponed any discussion until much later, over sushi and sake.

One of the Japanese remarked that business development was like finding the right seeds, planting them in the right place and watching them grow into trees, over time. This was quite lost on the American Vice-President, in charge of business development, who could only concentrate on the figures. The gardening-metaphor Japanese told Ron later that the VP was merely an accountant – implying that, while he might be good at counting seeds, they would never germinate under his supervision; so there would never be trees, let alone fruit to harvest.

In the top right quadrant, we find the UK and Ireland, where people come over as very informal in their use of language but, once again, be aware of the unsaid in their conversation, which they will expect you to understand by their tone of voice and physiology; for example the statement: *'I hear you had a meeting with Jones'* doesn't expect the answer, *'Yes, I did'*. It expects an explanation for, or a description of the meeting. And it's worth bearing in mind the theory that the Irish are so polite that they'll always tell you what they think you want to hear.

The bottom left quadrant is pretty easy to understand: the Dutch, Germans and Swedes will not beat around the bush, they'll give it to you straight, but they will maintain their formality.

In the bottom right quadrant, by contrast, we find the US and Australia. Conversation is easy, straight to the point and pretty informal: the whole nine yards and no messing about.

And, of course, all of the above depends on the situation, and on the place in the pecking order of the people involved.

Some comparisons

The table below compares conversations between USA and UK business people. Because they speak the same language, one could be forgiven for thinking that communication between the two nations would present no problems. But, as you can see, there is enormous potential for misunderstanding and impatience.

USA	UK
● Informal	● Formal
● Straight to the point	● Vague
● Don't like wasting time and money	● Don't like discussing money matters up front
● The relationship is less important	● The relationship is the key
● Contract usually solidified by lawyers	● Contract based on trust

Things can become even more complicated when English is the second or third language of one or more of the parties, and we go into this too in more detail in the chapter on language.

USA	FRANCE
● Less formal	● Very formal on the first encounter
● Straight to the point	● Change focus rapidly
● Don't like wasting time and money	● Need to understand the technical aspects first, and will need to discuss them at some length
● The relationship is less important	● The relationship is the key
● Contract usually solidified by lawyers	● Contract based on trust

The comparison above shows what to expect at a meeting between USA and French business people, where the French may communicate in English through an interpreter. As you will see, there are more similarities between the French and the English than there are between the UK and the US. Once again, beware of the 'unsaid'!

Diana's husband, Philip, worked on the Allied Staff in Berlin, which consisted of a mixture of Americans, French and Brits. Outsiders would say: 'oh, those poor French, they must feel so left out not speaking English'; but, in fact, the Brits and the French understood each other perfectly well; whereas no one understood most of the Americans, and vice versa.

USA	GERMANY
● Less formal	● Very formal on the first encounter
● Straight to the point	● Only interested in the business details
● Don't like wasting time and money	● Need to understand the technical aspects first and will express criticism openly
● The relationship is less important	● The relationship is the key
● Contract usually solidified by lawyers	● Contract is an extrapolation of trust

This comparison shows what happens when the US meets Germany: the Germans, like the French, will probably communicate in English with or without an interpreter. Germans are very punctilious with regard to detail, and they will remain very formal; this can give their counterparts the impression that they are cold and unfriendly. If they see/hear something that they think won't work, they'll say so (like many European cultures); they consider this to be purely practical, but it can be interpreted as antagonism. On the other hand, the Americans may be enthusiastic, which the Germans may interpret as a lack of sincerity.

The above are just a few examples to highlight some major cultural differences which can affect the first meeting. The chapter on 'Bloody Foreigners!' will give you more of a feel for possible misunderstandings.

The Dangerous Art of Mind-Reading

We all mind-read, because we like to know what other people are thinking; but mind-reading can frequently be very dangerous. When we find ourselves, or others, making assumptions about people from another culture, the most useful question we can ask is: *'How do you know?'* For example:

> 'They didn't like it.'
> 'How do you know?'
> 'They kept criticising?'
> 'What did they say?'
> 'They said the packaging wouldn't work for them?'
> 'How do you know that that means that they didn't like the product?'
> 'Well ....'

The answer is that they don't know any such thing. They have just put their own interpretation on a probably valid statement: packaging in one country doesn't always work in others.'

First Impressions Exercise

Supposing we come away from our first meeting with X feeling that maybe we didn't handle it as well as we would have liked, here are some useful questions we can ask ourselves.

Would it have been easier if X had:

1. been dressed differently?
2. looked different? (i.e. had a decent haircut, had better teeth, wore more/less make-up, had skin of a different colour, etc.)   cont.

---

3. behaved differently (i.e. didn't eat with bare hands, didn't use chopsticks, didn't put his feet on table, didn't burp after a meal, didn't gesture so much when talking, etc.)
4. stood closer to/further away from us?
5. had a tidier office?

In other words, what was it that we saw that put us off our stride and stopped us from being at our best? If none of the above relates to our situation, we can ask ourselves: 'what would have made it easier?'

Once we are aware of what it is that puts us off, we can also be aware that what people look like and how they behave, has nothing to do with who they are.

If there is nothing in the above that relates to us in this situation, the next set of questions relate to what we heard.

Would it have been easier if X had, for example:

1. been more direct?
2. a better command of the language?
3. spoken less formally?
4. kept to the point?
5. not overloaded us with detail?
6. been less bombastic?

Once again, we need to find out what it was that put us off. What would have made it easier? If, having asked ourselves the question, we realise that - for example - we felt our time was wasted discussing detail that didn't concern us, we can tell X next time that he/she needn't worry about all that, because someone else deals with that side, and we can elegantly steer the conversation to matters that do concern us.

We can't change other people

What we can do is change our own responses to their behaviour. Suppose we like to work in an immaculate office and X's office is like a tip, which offends our sensibilities; the question we could ask ourselves might be: *is it useful to respond by being offended, or would it be simpler to accept the fact that this is the way that X likes to work?*

Or, suppose we like lots of eye contact and X doesn't look at us, which makes us feel uncomfortable, the question is: what is actually happening, and what effect is this having on us?

Maybe we feel that the fact that X doesn't look at us means that X doesn't respect us, or maybe we have interpreted X's behaviour as having something to hide. This is a perfect example of the dangers of mind-reading. There are dozens of reasons why X might not be looking at us: maybe X is primarily auditory (see below), and is paying us the courtesy of turning his best ear towards us – all the better to hear us with; or maybe, in X's culture it is disrespectful to look people in the eye until one knows them better – to name but two (in Japan, for example, one avoids eye contact 90% of the time). One thing is sure, we have no evidence at this stage that X doesn't respect us – we've made it up.

Once we change the way we respond, the world changes round us. We open ourselves up to possibilities that weren't there before.

Did we speak the same language?

Do you ever come away from a meeting feeling as though you've been talking to a brick wall? Wherever in the world we are hoping to trade, we will find people who have programmed their brains in different ways. Some of us think best by creating pictures in our mind's eye; some of us do it by creating sounds in our mind's ear; and some of us process our thoughts best through our feelings, and our language reflects how we are thinking.

- For example, phrases like: *'from my point of view'*, *'Look!'*, *'Let's get this into perspective'*, *'I see what you mean,'* all contain visual references, and show us that the person is in **visual mode**, and thinking in pictures.
- Whereas *'Listen!'*, *'that rings a bell'*, *'that sounds like a good plan'*, *'it struck a chord'*, all relate to sound: we can hear that they are in **auditory mode**, and thinking with their mind's ear.
- People who process their thoughts through their bodies will say things like: *'a sticky situation'*, *'I couldn't grasp what he was saying'*, *'it was very touching'*, *'my feeling is …'*; they're getting through to us with the help of their **feelings**.
- And, of course, people will use their other two senses – **taste and smell**: *'I smell a rat!' 'follow your nose'*, *'sugaring the pill'*, *'a bitter argument.'*

The trick is to speak the same language as them, rather than expecting them to understand yours. For example, if someone says: *'Listen! I can't understand this'* – there's no point in *showing* them yet another picture: they're in auditory mode, so explain it to them verbally. (You'll find much more about language patterns in Diana's previous books – see bibliography.)

Start listening to what people are really saying: if you listen, they will tell you exactly how they are processing their thinking. If you get plenty of practice in everyday conversation, you'll find it much simpler when you get into business meetings. You can also listen to people talking on the car radio while you're travelling, and let them give you useful clues about how they're thinking.

Change your physiology – change your thinking

We talked earlier about copying the physiology of the people we are working with; this not only helps us to create rapport with them, it also helps to put us into the other person's thinking mode.

People in visual mode will sit fairly upright; their eyes will flash upwards as they are talking (to check the information in the picture files in their brains); their gestures will be at eye level; their voices will be fairly high-pitched; they will breathe high in their chests, and they will talk fast – to keep up with the pictures in their mind's eye.

At the other extreme, people in kinaesthetic (jargon for thinking through one's feelings) mode will have a more rounded physiology; they will use their stomachs for breathing; their voices will be much deeper and slower than visual people's; their gestures will be at body level; and they will look down (generally towards the hand they write with), to check out your propositions out with their feelings. It takes more time to process one's thinking through one's body, so the responses to your questions may come slowly. Next time you try to have a conversation with an upset child, who is feeling hurt, you'll understand why you have to wait so long for an answer: when you're stuck in your feelings, words aren't that easily available.

It's useful to be aware that visual and kinaesthetic people can drive each other mad (unless they realise what's happening): the kinaesthetics may feel that the visuals are hustling them; while, to the visuals, the kinaesthetics can appear to be deliberately obtuse.

People in auditory mode will come in between the two extremes: their physiology will be more relaxed than the visuals, but less rounded that the kinaesthetics; they will breathe using their rib cages; their voices will be mid-range; their gestures will be at ear/neck level, and they will talk slower than the visuals. They will get their information by looking towards one ear or the other, which is where they have filed their auditory information.

There's another auditory mode: auditory digital. People in this mode will be thinking in binary: yes or no; right or wrong; black or white. In this mode, there is no middle way. These people will generally look down towards the hand they don't write with, to check out information in their internal files.

Of course, we all use all of our senses, but most of us have a favourite. Which of the above is yours? And which are your friends? Try taking on the physiology of someone completely unlike you, and discover what changes inside you when you do. To prove to yourself that this works, try an experiment – think of something that really depresses you, and then walk round the room looking up at the ceiling. Can you go on feeling depressed?

Depression is all about feelings: if you are looking up, you are in visual mode, and detached from your feelings, so they can't affect you.

Watch television, and see how people's eyes move to access the information they have filed in their brains. Do some more manwatching. Experiment with other physiologies: copy the way other people use their bodies: this will put you on the same wavelength; you'll see eye to eye and you'll find that he or she is on your side. Taking on someone else's walk is interesting: visual people will walk with their feet parallel; auditory people walk with their toes slightly turned out, to pick up any sounds around them; and kinaesthetic people will walk with their feet well turned out, really in touch with the ground (ballet dancers will give you an excellent example of this). Try out a mode that isn't yours, and discover what changes in your thinking, and in your connection to the outside world.

Different thinking produces different behaviour at meetings

Here is a very interesting graph (Figure 3.4 opposite), borrowed from the Glasgow NLP Trainer John McWhirter.

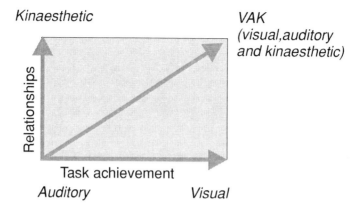

*Fig 3.4 – The thinking needed to achieve the task,
while maintaining the relationship*

Different thinking creates different agendas:

- People in visual mode can behave like gaze hounds: they'll see their quarry, and they'll go for it. No amount of calling, whistling, blackthorn or barbed wire will deflect them from their task. They'll achieve their objective at any price, and probably make enemies along the way, as the question of rapport never crosses their minds.
- People in kinaesthetic mode, at the other extreme, will be going for rapport at any price; so they may simply waste time working on the friendship side, and fail to achieve the task.
- People in auditory mode will be 'going by the book': for them the rules are all-important, and they may spend so much time concentrating on the right way of doing things that they achieve neither rapport nor the task.

The trick here is to be aware of how people are thinking, so that we can be flexible enough to think their way, join them in their model of the world, and then lead them out of it; so that we can both create the relationship and achieve the task.

As you will see from Figure 3.4, thinking in only one way will achieve only one thing: we need to be able to use our visual, auditory and kinaesthetic skills to achieve the task, maintain the relationship and get the fine detail right.

Both the physical and the behavioural sub-auras can be pretty important at the first encounter; but, once the relationship has been established, and one has moved into Friendly Business or Friendly Personal, neither of these matters, because the inner layers relate more to personal than to cultural values.

Armed with the information now in your possession, you will realise that the first impressions that you get from others are simply information: if you find yourself doing business, for example, with a woman in a chador in Iran, with a Texan in a cowboy outfit, with a Jew wearing a yarmulke, you know that these are just people who are dressed according to their culture. And if you find yourself sitting on the ground, eating with your fingers and being offered a sheep's eye, you can appreciate the openness and generosity of these people who are inviting you, as an honoured guest, to share the behaviour of their culture.

Success Checklist

1.   The physical and behavioural sub-auras exert more influence at the first meeting.

2.   Modify your dress according to the culture you are in.

3.   Notice if anything you see puts you off your stride.

4.   Notice if anything you hear puts you off your stride.

5.   Anything that affects you in these auras is about behaviour, and has nothing to do with who this person is.

6.   Notice the language (or lack of) within the language.

7.   Mind-reading can be dangerous.

8.   We can't change other people, but we can change our responses to them.

9.   Speak the same language.

10. Change your physiology - change your thinking.

4

Coming Up Against Brick Walls – The Sub-auras – Part II:

3. The Technical Sub-aura

The Technical Sub-aura relates to our knowledge, capability and intelligence. It is the centre of our knowledge, our experience and our ongoing education or learning. It represents the information we have gathered over the years and is responsible for converting and processing this into solutions. And, as you will discover later, it is equally powerful in whatever aura it is located.

This section is divided into two parts: 'us' and 'them'. In the first part we use Ron's IOTM (Input-Output Translation Mechanism) model, which shows us how we can access and process information that is of a higher quality than we have already, in order to seek better solutions.

The second part looks at the culture we are about to visit, to give us some ideas in advance about where they might be on the scale between open-mindedness and tunnel vision. In other words, it will help us to predict the sort of responses we can expect from them to any proposals we might make: will they be interested in, or horrified by, the thought of trying something different?

Us

Figure 4.1 (overleaf) shows our problem-solving mechanism. When we have a problem to solve, or a project to mastermind, we retrieve the relevant information from the store in our brains, we apply it to the problem or project in question, and come up with a solution. In other words, the input is our knowledge (however it was acquired) and, when applied to the problem, it is translated into output, i.e. the solution.

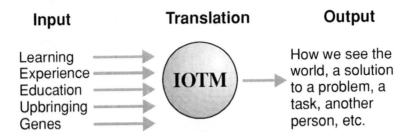

Fig 4.1 – The Input-Output Translation Mechanism

It is at this stage that we need to remember that the solution we are producing is a result of our experience and knowledge, together with our upbringing, education and genes, and ours alone. Our colleague, as a result of entirely different input, will have a different model of the world from ours, and our solution may not appeal to him, or it may not work in his country, or it may not fit in with the image of his company; there are dozens of reasons why our solution might not be suitable for him or her.

Well before we find ourselves at an impasse, a useful strategy is to increase our own input by using other perceptual positions – as well as our own. Let's imagine that our prospective business partner (we'll call him or her 'A') has a problem about our doing business together, and we need to come up with a solution. Remembering that all we can bring to bear upon this problem is our own knowledge and experience, we can expand our usefulness and creativity by looking at it from different points of view.

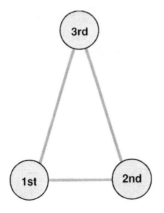

The perceptual positions in Figure 4.2 are numbered according to the grammatical classification for personal pronouns:

● 1st position (I) is me and my awareness of the situation

● 2nd position (you) is 'if I were you'

● 3rd position (he/she) is the outsider: the detached analyst

Fig 4.2 – Perceptual Positions

Step 1. Stand in a spot (which we shall call 1st position) where you can think about the problem solely from your point of view, and apply all your knowledge and experience to finding a solution. When you have everything you need, step out of that spot, and leave all the thinking that goes with it behind you.

Step 2. Shaking off any remaining thoughts as you go, move to the 2nd position spot, opposite where you've been standing (see Figure 4.2). This is where you step into A's shoes: where you become A, and experience everything from his or her perspective. If you take on A's physiology and gestures, you will find yourself thinking more like he or she does. Use all your senses to become A: see what A sees; hear what A hears; feel what A feels; taste what A tastes and smell what A smells; discover how A is responding to this problem: is he or she for your proposal or against it and, if the answer is 'against it', why? What's going inside A that produces this answer?

Then, you can apply A's self to the problem, as if he or she wants to find a solution; and see what A comes up with. When you have everything you need by way of input for A, step out of that spot, and leave all the thinking that goes with it behind you.

(NB: if at any stage, you find yourself thinking your thoughts, rather than A's, in this positions, move back into 1st position, deal with those thoughts, and then step back into 2nd and go back to being A again.)

Step 3. Shaking off any remaining thoughts as you go, move into 3rd position: the spot at the apex of the triangle – well away from the other two positions; lean back and fold your arms. You are now the detached outsider, observing both solutions disinterestedly and dispassionately. From this position, you will be able to analyse where both those people are coming from, and you will also be able to see what will work for both of them, and what won't. From this position, you can also make modifications to both plans, and create a solution that will please everybody. (The same applies to 'out of place thoughts' from this position: if something comes to you from your self or A, move back into that position – returning to 3rd only for observer thoughts.)

Step 4. Now, equipped with your new knowledge and your new solution, go back to 1st position and, in your imagination run the movie of the new solution taking place. Use all your senses as you watch it, and ask yourself these questions:

Does it work?
Does it fit in with the way I like to do business?
Does it fit in with the way my company likes to do business?
And any other questions that may come up. Make a mental note of
any reservations.

Step 5. Move into to 2nd position again, leaving your self behind, and run
the movie as if you were A, asking the same questions.
Does it work?
Does it fit in with the way I like to do business?
Does it fit in with the way my company likes to do business?

If each of you is happy with the solution, then you're in business; if there are
any reservations on either side, go back to 3rd position, re-analyse the
solution according to the new information that has come up, and modify it
again. Then repeat Steps 4 and 5. You can redo the complete triangle, if
necessary, until both sides are happy.

The great advantage of literally doing this exercise in different positions
on the ground is that we separate our thoughts into the areas where they really
belong. If we do it sitting in a chair, we may get unhelpful interference and
noise from niggles swirling about in the wrong places. You will also astonish
yourself by the increased value of your own perception of the problem, once
you have added the information from the other two positions; and both A and
A's company will be impressed at the surface level by your business acumen
and flexibility, and at the deeper mental sub-aura level (we come to this aura
later in the chapter), which is less conscious and more powerful.

If you play around with this exercise, on the ground, with any problems
or disagreements you might have with other people, you'll discover how
effective it is. Then, once you've got the feeling of how it works, you'll be
able to do it in your head – should you find yourself needing to do it on the
spot, at a meeting for example.

To illustrate the advantages of enhanced input, let's invent two
accountants, X and Y.

X knows accounting backwards: it is, after all, just number crunching –
and can be applied to any business. His task is to produce a financial
forecast. His input consists of the figures obtained from past experience; the
translation is an extrapolation into the future; the output is a spreadsheet
showing figures in some sort of a Profit and Loss (P/L) Account, based
solely on his past experience and the little information he has acquired over
the years.

Y, on the other hand, not only has a sound understanding of the business, he also retrieves information from the sales, marketing, distribution and other departments, as well as from outside sources, such as market trends. Y's P/L Account will bear little resemblance to X's (See figure 4.4).

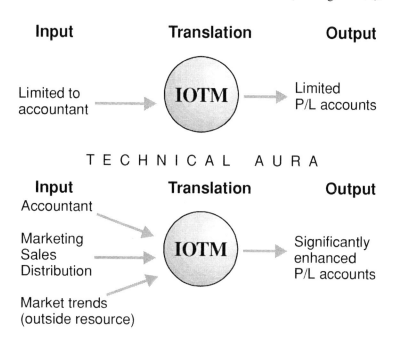

Fig 4.3 – Different IOTM according to X and Y

The technical aura defines the rate at which people are able to transform their knowledge into practice. It defines whether people have an open mind or whether they have tunnel vision.

To go back to our accountants: X is totally associated with his or her technical aura and its content; he is so involved in his technical aura that he knows he doesn't need external input. Y, on the other hand, is aware that there is always masses more to learn, so he can dissociate at any stage, and shift perceptual positions freely, whenever he wants to enhance the information he already has.

Bateson maintained that no data are every truly raw. We apply our own bias – whether this be from education or culture – to everything we learn. So, one of the greatest favours we can do ourselves is to pretend occasionally that we know nothing. If we know nothing, any input of information into our databank can remain reasonably raw.

The greater the input we receive from different sources (whether these be from the country itself or back home), the better the quality of our output; and the exercises we give you will open up your minds to even more possibilities.

What we get from all this effort is the most elegant solution to the problem; a solution that will be acceptable to as many people as possible. We also get a lot of kudos from A and A's company, creating the ambience for a long-term productive business relationship.

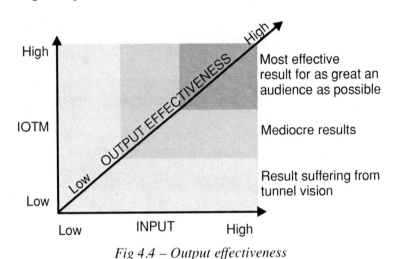

Fig 4.4 – Output effectiveness

Figure 4.4 explains how the ratio of information used, multiplied by the IOTM (or the effectiveness by which this information is translated into a solution), enhances the effectiveness of our outcome. In other words the more sources of knowledge that we have, and the more effectively we can turn this knowledge into a solution, the greater our success will be.

We can use different perceptual positions and the IOTM model for all aspects of international business – as well as at home and at play – when we need a solution that will satisfy other people as well as ourselves.

Them

Figure 4.5 can be used to help analyse the country we are going to visit, to give us more idea of what to expect from its people in the technical aura. It is based on two questions:

- Do they have the same opportunities to access information as we do?
- Do they have the ability to process this information and come up with a solution?

These factors are definitely influenced by environment and culture; but, as always, we need to keep our own minds open, and be aware that the individual we are about to meet will not always be typical of his or her culture.

Information

This relates to the acquisition and awareness of the up-to-date knowledge of all the business aspects in a particular culture – for instance, financial transactions, technical systems, the latest new laws relating to business and so on.

As an example, in certain countries around the world, readily available information is limited – due, for instance, to governmental restrictions. Therefore the people might just not have enough information to solve problems effectively. For our analysis, it is fairly easy to identify whether the appropriate information is available in the country we are to visit by checking the sources listed in Chapter 1.

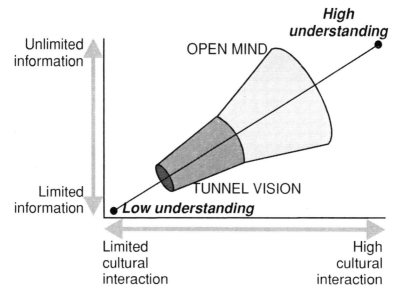

Fig 4.5 – Tunnel-vision versus open-mindedness

Understanding

Information is worthless unless one knows how to use it. By 'understanding' we mean the ability to use one's knowledge to create output. In other words, the latest high tech gadgetry is wasted on us if we don't know how to use it. From Figure 4.6, we can see that, where there is limited information, limited cultural interaction and low understanding, vision will be strictly limited; whereas, at the other extreme, vision is dramatically expanded.

Cultural interaction

This relates to the connection and communication that these people have with other cultures, which is not always easy to measure. But, if we take an isolated country, we can expect its people to have a tendency towards the bottom left corner. They appear to have little interaction with other cultures, and thus will probably not understand how other cultures might act in certain aspects of life or business. On the other hand, a country with open boundaries, and a high level of education and information, will have a tendency towards the top right.

> Ron met an entertaining Muscovite who had spent many years living in different West European countries. As one of the few Russians at that time to experience such a way of life, he appreciated the power of cultural impact. He told Ron that, when he went home to Russia, the locals told him over and over again that money was up for grabs in the West. His explanation to them was that, in Russia, people get paid whether they solve a problem or not; whereas, in the West, people might have to solve a hundred problems a day or face the sack. This explanation probably fell on deaf ears – people don't appreciate having their theories ruined.

Like all our analyses, this one is just to help you to form a picture of the overall situation of the country you are about to visit.

4. The Mental sub-aura

We're now going to think about the mental sub-aura, and the interaction between it and the physical one.

The mental sub-aura covers our personality, emotions, values and integrity. We become more aware of the importance of this aura when we get into Friendly Business, and even more as we get into Friendly Personal and Inner-Core.

When we meet someone for the first time, the first question we may ask ourselves is: *'Can I build a relationship with this individual?'* And we need to remember that our preconceived ideas may influence this decision. We also need to be aware of how we know that we do, or don't, want to build this relationship. Is it what they look like? Or what they sound like? Or what they say? Or what they do? Or is it something completely different?

As we realised earlier, our first impressions of someone from another culture can be very misleading. We talk about 'gut feelings', or 'a feeling in our bones', and it is the structure of this supposed instinctive understanding that we are exploring, so that once you know what it is, you can apply it for yourself.

As we are still preparing for our first meeting, and are aware that it is the outer auras that are most influenced by culture, we are taking immense care with our preparations.

So, before we go any further, let's try a First Impressions Experiment (you'll need a pencil and paper).

1. Think about someone you met on business, and liked at once.

2. Remember how soon you were able to discuss personal things like your families.

3. Remember how soon you were able to discuss more personal things.

4. Think about what you said and did to create this relationship.

5. Think about what the other person said and did to create the relationship.

6. Think about how you were thinking about the other person.

Then think about a business colleague/partner you did not take to, and ask yourself the same questions.

If you compare and contrast your answers relating to the two different people, you will discover that the structure is quite different. The most interesting differences will be your responses to Question No 6: how you were thinking about the other person, and Question No 4: what you said and did to create the relationship. What the other person said and did will have been in direct response to your behaviour.

What was your gut feeling, on each occasion? Or, if you operate visually and don't do gut feelings, what was your intuition? How were you thinking about these two people? Were you just accepting the person you liked as who he or she was? And, if so, what would have happened with the person you didn't like, if you had just accepted who he or she was? What difference would it have made to the ongoing relationship?

Alternatively, you could reverse the questions and ask yourself what difference it would have made to the first relationship if you had thought about the first person in the way you were thinking about the second person.

John Grinder, the co-creator of NLP, blew Diana's mind on the first day she spent with him. Participants worked in pairs with people they didn't know, and pretended that they were old school friends who were catching up on news. Then everyone wrote down five adjectives to describe the person they had just been talking to. Diana wrote that Simon was: intelligent, amusing, sparky, engaging and fun. For the second half of the exercise, John told each person awful things about the other and sent them back to talk to each other again. Then they had to describe their partner once more. Diana wrote that Simon was: pompous, arrogant, and unpleasant.

The sudden realisation that she had written such entirely different things about the same person knocked her previous thinking that relationships 'just happened' into a cocked hat. She had to do some serious rethinking.

So what is the relationship between the technical aura and the mental one? The technical aura is responsible for the processing of information, and equates with Capabilities in the logical levels. The mental one relates to Beliefs, Values and Integrity, as well as Identity, and is thus of much higher importance. Of the two, the technical sub-aura is maintained at a fairly conscious level – in other words, knowing what we know; whereas, the mental-sub aura, like our beliefs and values, has been with us so long and is so deeply ingrained, that we may be unaware at a conscious level of how it affects us.

Let's see how this works with our IOTM model.

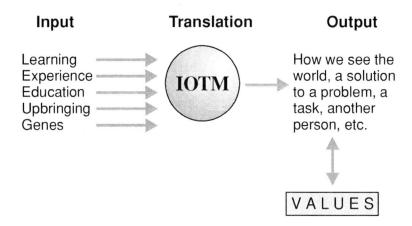

Input	Translation	Output
Learning		How we see the
Experience	IOTM	world, a solution
Education		to a problem, a
Upbringing		task, another
Genes		person, etc.

VALUES

Figure 4.6 – IOTM and Values

Figure 4.6 reminds us that, once we obtain a solution to our problem, we then need to square this solution with the Beliefs, Values and Integrity of both parties. To illustrate how easy it is to mess things up in other people's Mental Sub-auras, let's suppose that we have shaken hands on a deal in the USA; the next phase here would be to bring in the lawyers and sign a contract. In other countries, the handshake is probably worth more than any written agreement because, for them, to renegue on a handshake is the ultimate dishonour, and the reneguer would lose face in his or her community.

If, as an American company, we bring in a lawyer in a country where the handshake is all that is required to seal a contract, this not only goes against the cultural customs of the country, it is also a denial of understanding of the intrinsic values of the person we have struck the deal with. We have (albeit unintentionally) just swept his intrinsic values aside, and considered him untrustworthy (Identity level). The deal that was in the bag is off – and we have no one to blame but ourselves.

The Germans have an excellent expression: '*Fingerspitzengefühl*' – literally a 'feeling in the tips of your fingers,' it is the instinctive understanding and appreciation of a situation; and it is *Fingerspitzengefühl* that we need to operate effectively in the Mental Sub-aura.

Let's take another example. Market research shows that the market for our product has vast potential in a country where the people will have little understanding of what we have to offer them. We have done all the exercises and established that it will sell if we do things properly.

We are now invited to give a presentation to a company, and have been told that the Chairman will be there. However he may come across, the Chairman is the Chairman and, in principle, without his support our cause is lost. So, before we do anything else, we need to acknowledge who he is as Chairman, and who he is as a person, as well as his personal beliefs and values. So we start by asking him some polite questions, rather than by presenting our product. Once he realises that we are safe to deal with, we can begin our step by step explanation of what our product is about. (We shall discuss this process further later on.)

> As an example of the above, Ron was in Iran to present a product: a liquid, which, with other nutrients, would produce a final product for consumption. This product was new to this market; they had had experiences with other liquids, but these were quite unlike Ron's.
>
> Ron did his homework: he gathered all the information he could get hold of to do the IOTM exercise. He discovered that problems had arisen with the other liquids, and that the chairman had never heard of his particular product. Applying figure 4.6, the Chairman had limited information, limited understanding and limited cultural interaction.
>
> When they met, the Chairman – who by this time had been briefed – explained, in detail, why he knew Ron's product was never going to work: his experiments with other high viscosity products had resulted in failure; he was sorry Ron had wasted his time, etc, but ...
>
> As a result of his careful homework, Ron was able to tell the Chairman that he was absolutely right – that he knew that there had been problems with other products. Result: Chairman looks well-informed and astute in front of his staff, feels good, thinks Ron's an unusually intelligent westerner and is now prepared to eat out of his hand.
>
> Ron then had all the time in the world to explain to him step by step what the differences were between his product and the others they had worked with, and why he would not have any problems with what Ron had to offer.

We have chosen this story as an example of how to create a paradigm shift. The Chairman's paradigm was that there was no way this proposal could work; Ron's was that this product was very successful in other countries. And people will rarely shift their paradigms if they don't feel safe: they're concentrating so hard on protecting themselves that they can't expand their minds in any direction, let alone change them. In NLP terms, this could be described as joining the other person in their model of the world, and then leading them into an even better one.

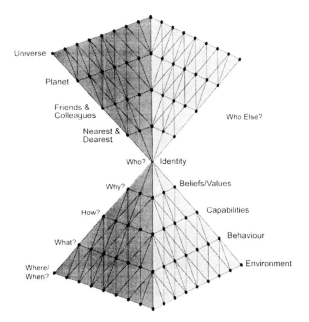

Fig 4.7 – Gregory Bateson's Logical Levels of Thinking

We can't solve a problem at the level at which it was created

Logical levels again! The problem here is at belief level: Ron believes his product will work; the Chairman believes it won't, and they could argue fruitlessly from their own positions until the cows came home.

So the solution is to move up a level or two. Ron creates rapport at identity level by acknowledging that the Chairman is absolutely right, and this takes matters up to the 'Who Else' level: the company looks good because their Chairman looks good. He is now in a position to create his hybrid paradigm, whereby he comes over as credible, and the Chairman comes over as someone with intelligent, valuable input. He created rapport with the mental-sub aura before addressing the technical sub-aura.

This man was to become Ron's very first customer in Iran.

Success Checklist

1. Get all the information you can lay hands on about the country and the company.

2. Use the IOTM to come up with solutions.

3. For a solution to please everyone, use different perceptual positions.

4. Gain some understanding of their technical sub-aura.

5. First impressions can be misleading.

6. Accept people for who they are.

7. Use your sensitivity to feel your way into the mental sub-aura, and keep yourself there.

8. Create and maintain rapport at identity level and above.

5

The Cultural Labyrinth

This isn't a proper labyrinth, but we're using it here because it looks like a brain. We are aware that we have led you down many winding paths and that, by now, you may be feeling that your brains are getting scrambled. To condense and settle the knowledge you have already acquired, you will find a proper labyrinth quite soon.

 Your brain is divided into two distinct parts: the left and the right. In general, the left brain controls the right side of the body, and the right side controls the left. The left brain is in charge of words, logic, and step-by-step thinking, whereas the right brain thinks without words, at a deeper level, and is in charge of our creativity and our responses to other people – among other things. They are connected by the corpus callosum, through which messages pass from one side to the other.

The problem with the left brain is that, because it is in charge of words and logic, it thinks it knows everything; and, because it controls the right side of the body, everything right is good, and everything that is not right is not good. In English, we talk about people being 'gauche' (French for 'left') if they are clumsy or tactless; we say things are 'sinister' (Latin for 'left') if they make us feel uncomfortable; whereas anything that is 'right' is good' or correct.

If we have been trained to think primarily with our left brains, we are going to believe that logical things, like the bottom line and the law, are all that matter in business, and that relationships and intangible values (which we come to later) have no relevance in a world that appears to be ruled by money.

But our two brains are like the two sides of a coin: each serves its own purpose. If we cut a gold coin in half across its width, it will only be worth its weight in gold; only if we leave it as it is, do we have buying power. Each side of our brain can only operate properly with the support of the other.

In this chapter we are going to look at some aspects of business and the effects of differences between cultures, and at what one might expect to experience in different situations.

Gregory Bateson (on whose thinking a lot of NLP is based), maintained that dealing with humans was about as predictable as playing snooker with mice instead of balls; in other words, if we hit a ball in a certain way, we can more or less predict the result. But, if we substitute mice for the balls, anything can happen.

If we add the extra ingredient of differences in culture, the possibilities instantly become even greater; so we need to be aware of what is going on in our business dealings before, during and after we put CAT into practice.

As we have seen, before we begin to do business abroad, some knowledge of the history of the country in question will be useful; but our most important asset will be the information we can get from people who have experienced doing business in this different culture. Another thing we can do, which we haven't mentioned before, is read novels and watch films about the country, which will give us a feel for the ambience.

At this stage, you may feel completely overwhelmed by information, so it's time for a break. Opposite is a copy of the labyrinth built into the stone floor of Chartres Cathedral, which the monks used to crawl round on their knees. It's a journey, a pilgrimage, a problem-solving device; it's whatever you want it to be. Diana has a theory that it works because there are so many twists and turns that it shifts us back and forth from left to right-brain thinking, and gets the corpus callosum (see above) working properly – with the result that both sides of the brain can work together to optimum effect.

What we'd like you to do now is to take the information you have read so far – even if you can't consciously remember it all, your mind has got everything recorded at an unconscious level. You might like to re-read the 'Success Checklists' at the end of Chapters 1 to 4, to bring the outlines back to your conscious mind. Just read through them quietly, as a gentle reminder; then, leaving outside the circle any doubts that you might have about the power of your memory, use your index finger to follow the path of the labyrinth into the middle. (Some people recommend using the left index finger.) The entrance is at the bottom and, as you will have realised, the thin

lines are just the ends of blocks of stone and the thick lines show you where to turn.

The difference between a labyrinth and a maze is that there is only one way in and out of a labyrinth. You can't get lost; so just allow yourself to relax and follow the path. You will find that there are seemingly endless twists and turns and one minute you're close to the centre, and the next you're on the edge. All this will serve to settle the information into both sides of your brain and body.

Take as long as you like, stopping whenever you feel like if a thought comes to you; and, when you get to the middle, spend as long as you like in there. Some people like to think of the middle as their deeper, wiser selves, and the outside as their relationship with the outside world. As you will see, the labyrinth divides easily into quadrants, and some people like to divide these quadrants into different aspects of what they are doing at the moment. The whole thing is just a metaphor – choose what you will, and explore.

When you have spent enough time in the middle to absorb what you have discovered, you can follow the path out again, at whatever speed you like, looking forward to the second half of the book.

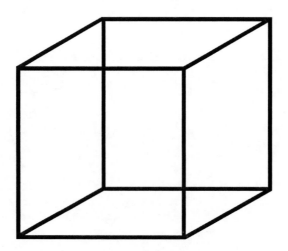

And now, before we move on, here is another metaphor for you to think about. Is this cube on the floor, or on the ceiling? In other words, are you looking down into the bottom left hand corner furthest away from you, or up into the top right hand corner furthest away from you?

Watch it for a bit, with your eyes defocused, and you will notice that it appears to move. The reason for this is that your brain is trying to make sense of the information that it has; and it has no background information about where to place the cube – so it just keeps on trying.

And the point of this exercise is just to demonstrate that your brain will always try to find the best solution; and that it's okay to be confused if you haven't got enough background information.

Back to business. Ron has a vast number of American friends on assignment in the UK. They all say that some of their bosses, at the level of president and vice-president, have difficulties in understanding that business is done differently abroad. This is not unique to the USA, it is a world wide problem, and our reason for writing this book.

The worst mistake we can make, when doing business abroad, is to apply the rules of the game, or paradigms, from back home. A typical example of this is Americans coming to the UK and assuming that, because there is a common language, things will operate in the same way. As we have already discussed, the Brits are more formal than the Americans and do not necessarily say what they mean. They also dislike being hustled. So, instead of admitting that they need more time before making a decision, they may say: 'it's very interesting. We'll pursue it'. The Americans return home, believing the deal done, and wonder why they never hear from the Brits again.

Another example is Ron's first meeting with two Japanese businessmen, who had come to discuss a topic which was of little interest to his company. Later they referred to another opportunity which was of the utmost interest; but, because the Japanese on the whole have a set agenda, this second topic was not to be discussed in detail. It wasn't until a later meeting that they got around to discussing the worthwhile topic.

The following graphs demonstrate cultural differences in formality, trust and decision-making. Combined, they will give you an overall understanding of various cultures' ways of thinking.

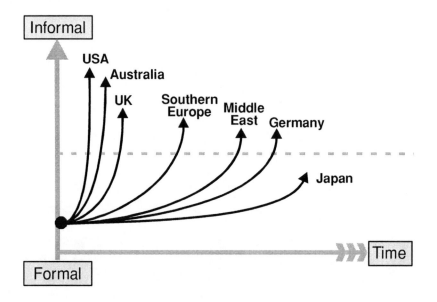

Fig 5.1 – Attitudes changing over time

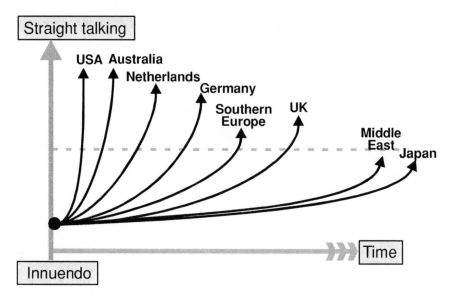

Fig 5.2 – Language used

In Figure 5.1 we can see the different lengths of time that are needed, in different cultures, for the move from the Formal Business Aura to Friendly Business. In the US, this move can happen very quickly, whereas in Japan it may take years: these two countries are the extremes. As we explored above, you can see that, although we may consider the Brits to be very close to the Americans, they need considerably more time before they are comfortable about moving to Friendly Business.

Figure 5.2 shows the way different cultures use language. The Americans prefer straight talk. They operate on a 'why waste time?' basis. This attitude will be found, to a lesser extent in most Scandinavian countries, the Netherlands and Germany (although it is never safe to assume that everyone in these countries will operate in the same way). As we move to the right, along the time line, and compare this diagram to figure 5.1, we see that we have to wait for the move to Friendly Business before the language becomes more straightforward, and we will have to wait a lot longer in Japan before we can expect clarity and precision.

To ensure that we have reached the clarity and precision that we need to do business effectively, it is always wise to ask our hosts to summarise their understanding of the process, during negotiation or presentation, in order to ensure that we have got our message across in the way we intended.

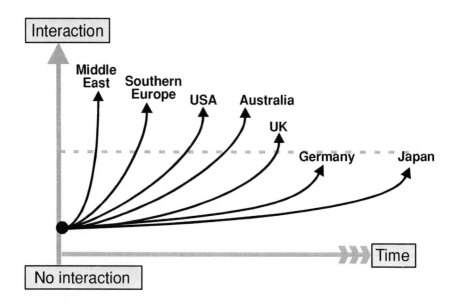

Fig 5.3 – Interaction during formal presentations

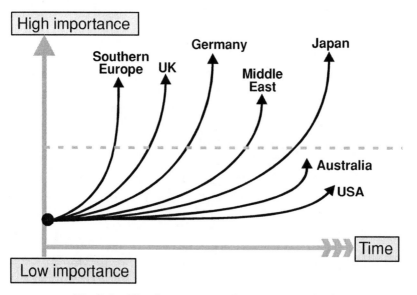

Fig 5.4 – The Importance of time in trust-building

Figure 5.3 shows what to expect when we are making or attending a formal presentation. At one extreme, in Japan, the audience will remain silent and will listen attentively, because it is not done to ask questions during a presentation, lest the presenter lose face. At the other extreme, people from the Middle East will be firing questions during the presentation, and even more afterwards. This may help to find a faster solution – but not necessarily.

Figure 5.4 summarises the differences in the time it can take to build trust in different culture, which we discussed in a previous chapter. As we saw, trust-building is the key to success in most cultures; it is of the least importance in the US where 'time is money', and of the most importance in Southern Europe, the UK, Germany and Japan. You will also notice that more time needs to be spent on trust-building in Japan, and less in Southern Europe. In some cultures it is important to visit and revisit the company, before trust is sufficiently established to take any action business-wise.

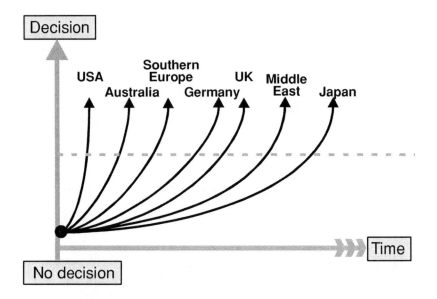

Fig 5.5 – The Importance of time in Decision Making

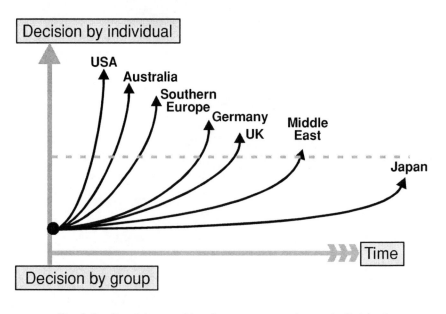

Fig 5.6 – Decision making by a group or by an individual

Figure 5.5 demonstrates how, in most cultures, decisions are not made until there is trust between the parties, and this may take time. Figs 5.4 and 5.5 support each other: 5.4 shows that trust-building is of low importance in the US and Australia, and this enables decisions to be made much faster than in, for instance, the Middle East (although there are occasions where decisions can be made more rapidly in here).

As you can see, decisions will take longer in Japan: this may also be due to 'ringi-sho', the written proposal that is first circulated among peers and then upwards for higher approval – whereas in the US one person may have the power to make the decision.

Figure 5.6 demonstrates how, in some cultures, decisions can be taken rapidly by an individual – whereas, in Japan, it must go to a group. But, once this group has agreed, the decision is made immediately.

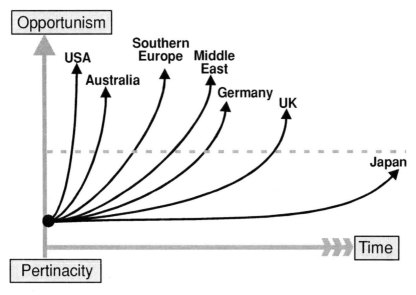

Fig 5.7 – Opportunism or pertinacity in decision making

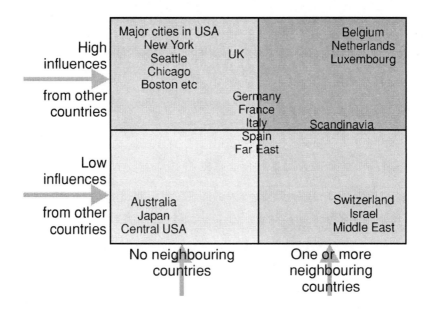

Fig 5.8 – Interaction with other countries

Fig 5.7 takes us back to Ron's first meeting with the two Japanese. We will remember that, because they had a set agenda, they were unable to discuss that second opportunity which was of particular interest to his company. The first topic was of no interest but, because the group decision had been made that that was the one to be discussed, they stuck to it with great pertinacity.

Proximity to and shared borders with other countries
(Figure 5.8 highlights these two parameters.)

Let's compare the state of Missouri – which is almost slap in the middle of the USA, with the country of Belgium – which is only one sixth of the size of Missouri.

To go 'abroad', the natives of Missouri have to do some serious travelling. It's a long way to Canada or to Mexico. They live in their own world, so the population is fairly homogeneous. Missouri is nicknamed 'The Show me State' – unless they've seen it, they won't believe it – and that's that.

Belgium, on the other hand, has three different cultures, with three different languages: the Walloons, the Flemish and a small group of German-speaking Belgians. For the Belgians, there is little effort involved in popping across the borders into The Netherlands, Germany, Luxembourg or France – so cultural diversity is the norm, whereas an influx from another country into Missouri could be considered very odd, and probably threatening. The other advantage that the Belgians have is their ability to speak several languages (essential for survival), and this means that they have more of a feel for different cultures (see Chapter 9, which is all about language).

Influence from other cultures
In big cities in the USA like New York and Chicago, whither migrants went in search of the excitements and the riches of the new world, people are more used to difference, so the influence from other cultures is high, and they are more adaptable. In big international cities, we may find it quicker and simpler to come up with business solutions that suit everybody. But, as there is no reason why business people from Missouri should understand

how business works in Europe, there is also no reason to expect that our paradigm would work for them, or theirs for us, come to that. And the same principle applies to paradigms from anywhere else in the world.

As we have already discussed, before we start thinking about doing business abroad, we need to be open to everything that makes a country tick: the legislation, the finance, the laws, the environment, the availability of raw materials, consumption trends, health consciousness, fuel costs and so on. These factors will vary around the world and are all-important additions to our databank of information.

The same is true for marketing, sales, distribution, and any other aspect of international business. Once we are aware of whereabouts on the chart these countries are, we will have more idea of what to expect by way of flexibility and openness to different ideas.

Some specific considerations
Many cultures have particular characteristics, so let's consider a few generalities.

- Some nations – for example, the former Eastern European countries, and some Middle Eastern countries – are, or were, suppressed by their governments, and therefore may have had limited interaction with other cultures.
- Limited interaction may also be due to the size of a country like the USA or Russia or the isolation of Japan, Australia or even the UK: countries surrounded by sea are, by their very definition, inclined to be insular.
- As a result, these nations may have little experience of the rest of the world, and how it works. Their information may therefore be biased and hence cause a kind of 'tunnel vision' when it comes to international matters as we saw in Chapter 2.
- In former times the Communist countries spoon-fed their inhabitants and told them that the West was decadent, imperialistic and so on. When the barriers were suddenly removed, these cultures had to adapt to 'Western' standards in order to survive in business. As we saw earlier, one relevant example of this change is that many managers of companies during the communist regime had no authority over finance, purchasing or pricing of goods. It was the Foreign Trade Office that was in charge of negotiating prices and contracts. Consequently, when the Iron Curtain came down, these managers had no feel for negotiating prices or

contracts, and little understanding of the financial side of business. And suddenly they found themselves in charge of all aspects of business.

● Another example is Iran. When the Islamic Revolution came in 1979, the Iranians were fed one-sided information about the perverted West. Of course a lot of them knew better, but we must never underestimate the consequences for the people of disinformation over a prolonged period of time.

● People come to believe things that they are told over and over again. While logic may tell them that the West is now safe to do business with, their earlier conditioning may leave them with deeper doubts, and these may take time and effort to assuage. Back to logical levels again – beliefs are high-level stuff so, once again, we need to create rapport at identity level and above, in order to change or modify them.

● The Cultural Auras will differ slightly for people from a vast or isolated country, which has limited interaction with other cultures/nations due to its sheer size, or miles of ocean – with little or no exposure to other cultures for a prolonged period of time.

● 'We are better than the rest of the world' syndrome
● Fear of losing control and power to outsiders
● One-sided or biased information (e.g. media, government, education, religion etc)

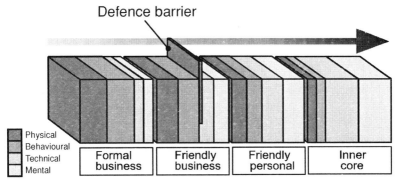

Fig 5.9 – Different influences create different defence barriers

We all need to keep ourselves safe from danger – whether this be real or imagined; and business people need to keep their companies safe, as well as themselves. If we look at Figure 5.9, we can see the kind of influences that create a sort of self-defence mechanism and add a barrier within the Friendly Business Aura between the Behavioural and Technical sub auras. If we are trying to build a relationship with business people who think they are better than the rest of the world, or who are afraid of losing control of the situation, or who have been fed disinformation, we may find ourselves being bounced off between the two auras. This sort of thing can happen in isolated cultures, like the Mid-West of the USA, and in the UK: one culture being isolated by land and the other by water.

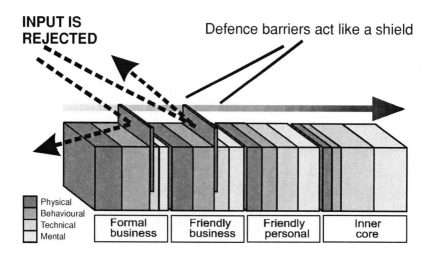

Fig 5.10 – Defence barriers rejecting inputs

Figure 5.10 shows us the defence barriers created by cultural fear, and applies to people who have a conscious or unconscious fear of any strangers who might know better than they do. (There is more about fear in the next chapter: 'The F*** Word'.) This is a cultural trait and there is nothing personal about it. To by-pass this fear, we need to be extremely diplomatic. We need to give the Brits respect: they need to feel important and especially knowledgeable. In other words, we're back to flexibility, using the Japanese Judo technique: 'Bend like a willow, do not break like a rose tree', and always remembering that if we overwhelm these people with knowledge, which they may not grasp up front, we will lose them.

We're now going to analyse CAT for people from a suppressed country or nation.

Influences
- One-sided or biased information (media, government, education, religion)
- Multi-level thinking suppressed
- Uncertainty

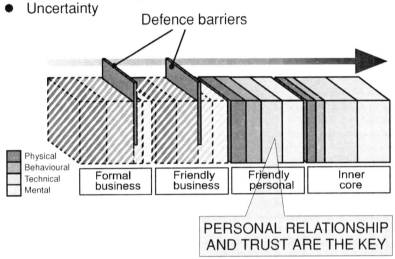

Fig 5.11 – CAT applied to suppressed cultures

People in these areas are either suspicious regarding business, or they are pretty remotely situated. Western business people could easily run rings round some of the managers who used to operate in the communist regime: those people who suddenly found themselves in control without having had a chance to get acquainted with different ways of doing business. Once again, we need to show these people great respect. Respect, as we have touched upon before, encompasses showing genuine care. Unless one is dealing with a bunch of crooks, it can do no harm, and both parties will get enormous benefit from it, because the Friendly Personal aura is much more important than the two business ones.

It is essential here to build a trusting relationship up front. So we ignore all business aspects initially, and focus on the relationship itself. The Formal Business and Friendly Business auras have been tainted by years of disinformation, so we simply by-pass them. Our first meeting, as described earlier, is simply a trust/relationship building exercise; once trust has been established, and only then, we can switch to business.

Once we have switched to business, we need to concentrate on creating a kind of symbiosis. In other words, this will be a joint venture, useful and profitable for both sides. We use our *Fingerspitzengefühl* and the utmost patience, because these people may not have our business and financial experience. We explain our ideas, and listen to theirs with particular attention; and we always compare notes to ensure understanding on both sides.

When we come to negotiating, we need to focus primarily on everything except finance, which will be discussed only when the time is right.

There are, of course, other subtle differences in the Cultural Auras around the world and these will be discussed in the chapters on 'Bloody Foreigners!'

Some notes on Hierarchy

Hierarchy is a cultural phenomenon as old as life on earth, and we've put it in here because it applies to countries as well as companies, and it's another useful overlay for our exploration of difference.

According to Douglas McGregor (1960) in his 'Theory X, Theory Y', there are two opposing beliefs about employees.

1. People are shiftless and lazy, and will not work unless they are made to.
2. People really like to work, and the job of the manager is to provide a working context, which will allow them to show what they can do.

There are three fundamental types of management.

1. At one extreme: the authoritarian (dictatorial, autocratic).
2. At the other extreme: the democratic (liberal, broad-minded)
3. 'Laisser-Faire': the principle of non-interference, which we shall ignore because – in our opinion – it doesn't work.

The dictatorial autocratic type has the following characteristics:

- fear of being overwhelmed by subordinates
- fear of losing control of power
- fear of passing on authority
- underestimates subordinates

- will take most if not all decisions him- or herself
- will not consult others
- supervises closely.

The liberal broad-minded type, in contrast:

- delegates as much responsibility to the lowest level as possible
- appreciates everybody's input
- will use the knowledge of subordinates to the maximum
- encourages subordinates to make decisions
- is not afraid of giving as much autonomy as possible to the lowest ranks
- makes decisions on the basis of group discussions
- makes requests, rather than giving orders
- expects co-operation.

Translated into CAT this shows distinct basic differences:

- Fear of being powerless
- Fear of being overwhelmed by subordinates and underestimating subordinates
- Fear of passing authority to the lowest level possible
- Will take most, if not all, decisions him- or herself

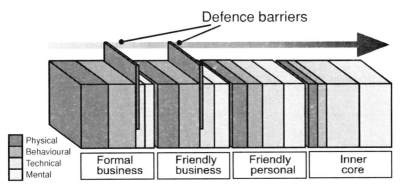

Fig 5.12 – CAT and the dictatorial type

Figure 5.12 shows us the dictatorial type, with strong defence barriers between the Behavioural sub-aura and the Technical sub-aura, in both the Formal Business aura and the Friendly Business aura. These people are usually surrounded by 'Yes' Men, who are afraid of losing their modicum of control. Political correctness is all-important, and this may undermine the creativity of the people, let alone the company. Under this type of management, the survival of a company in difficult times cannot be guaranteed.

● Give as much authority and autonomy to the lowest level possible
● Appreciate the input of others and use the knowledge of the subordinates
● Encourage the subordinates to take decisions

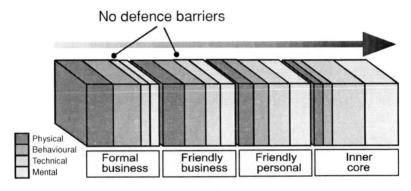

Fig 5.13 – CAT and the liberal type

At the other extreme, figure 5.13 shows how the liberal, broad-minded, mentoring managers operate: they have no defence barriers, because they are in control – so they don't need them.

This type of management is ideal in all situations, as long the managers remain consistent, and remember that ownership of a dog means that they don't have to do the barking.

Both types will thrive in the good times; but, in times of recession, the dictatorial autocratic type will hide behind past successes, whereas the mentoring type will generate an atmosphere of creativity.

These two types can be found throughout the world, and there are also some typical cultural types of management of which we need to be aware.

● In France we may find formal autocratic managers. A one-time CEO of the carmaker Renault reminded Ron of General de Gaulle's *'La France, c'est moi'*, when he presented a paper in the early 1990s at one of the

European Parliament workshops. He said that Renaults were as good as Japanese cars in every way, and technically they were far superior; he could not understand why the sales of Renaults were down, whereas the sales of Japanese cars were increasing significantly. This attitude is common in France, and many foreign companies operating in France have to change the names of their subsidiaries to something sounding French.

- In Germany, management has become somewhat more liberal, especially in the last two decades, but it remains formal and very structured: *'Ordnung muss sein'*. The Germans on the whole fear chaos and therefore rules are to be obeyed in order to maintain order.

- In the Netherlands, they have liberal management, but this is often undermined by jealousy. A favourite Dutch expression is: *'Het is moeilijk om de zon te zien schijnen in andermans water'* (freely translated: 'It is difficult to see the sun shine in someone else's water'). In other words, I am your boss and I drive a Skoda – while you drive a company BMW. I am jealous: I want a BMW, but I don't want to do your sales job. Another favourite expression: *'Voor een dubbeltje op de eerste rij zitten'* ('To sit in the front row for a dime') means to want the privileges, without being prepared to invest in them. Neither of these expressions seems to have an equivalent in other cultures. There's an even ruder expression about dimes (which we won't teach you), and this is illustrated by the story of the vice-president of a multinational who – without consulting – sent a memo to all the secretaries within the company telling them to refrain from using coloured paper-clips, as they were more expensive than the plain ones. Having omitted to consult, he was unaware that coloured paper-clips were used in order to make filing more efficient – thereby saving the company valuable time and money.

- Under authoritarian management, rank is of crucial importance, and you will often find in the United States that a subordinate who has had a brilliant idea has to make sure that it is his boss who gets the credit.

- In Japan, formality and rank are essential. Nonetheless there are some examples of a more liberal management. The founder of Sony, Akio Morita, followed the principals outlined by Tom Peters in the book he wrote many years later: MBWA (Managing by Wandering Around). He used to visit Sony subsidiaries and wander around, introducing himself to people by name only. He would then ask them about how they felt about life within the corporation and its overall management. They had no idea he was the CEO, and he got some very valuable feedback.

Whatever management system we find ourselves in, we now have the awareness and the flexibility to provide these people with what they need. Remember, hierarchical managers are basically frightened of losing face, of trouble from their bosses, of losing control and so on. Make them feel safe and important – unlike Diana's friend Art, who worked on contract for just such a company, and has no time for other people's airs and graces. When he arrived late one morning, and was greeted with a furious: 'you should have been here at nine o'clock!', his response was: 'Why? What happened?'.

Now that you know what to look for, and what to expect, you'll find it's much simpler to gauge where you are in the Cultural Auras, and how to behave, at any stage of your negotiations, wherever you might be in the world.

Success Checklist

1. People are not predictable

2. A common language doesn't mean that we'll understand each other

3. The time it takes to relax the formality, create trust and make decisions will vary according to culture.

4. Ask the question: is this culture isolated, or does it have lots of contact with other cultures?

5. We need to move up to a higher level of thinking to change other people's beliefs

6. Cultural influences can create barriers between the Behavioural and Technical Sub-Auras

7. Hierarchy can play an important part in the way people behave

8. We need different responses to the autocrat and the liberal management types

---

6

The 'F*** Word'

People, on the whole, don't like change; and, in international business, we are constantly confronted with the 'new and different', varying from dress codes all the way to financial transactions. When all this newness and difference doesn't fit in with our database of how the world works, it can throw us off balance, and create **fear** of the unknown.

We're going to think about two kinds of fear:

1. **Individual fear**: fear of flying, fear of enclosed spaces, fear of talking on the phone, fear of other people, fear of rejection, and so on.
2. **Cultural individual collective fear**: fear in an individual, a group of people or even a nation (e.g., fear of joining the Single European Currency, fear of trying a new unproven product, fear of breaking the rules, fear of taking a calculated risk, fear of making mistakes, etc.). Note that 'culture' in the context of this chapter is related to a nation, a company or a group of people. The media play a large part in creating and sustaining cultural fear – both in oppressed countries and supposedly free countries.

Individual fear

As this book is about business, we'll leave phobias for another day, but we'll spend some time thinking about one of the classic NLP questions: 'What stops us?'

How many times have you known exactly what you 'should' do in a given situation, but blown it nonetheless? Join the club, you're a member of the human race. Instruction books are all very well for robots, but they don't always work for people – they tell you what to do, but not how to do it.

So what stops us from being at our best at all times? What stops us from keeping our cool? What stops us from remembering what we were supposed to do? The answer is nearly always 'fear'.

Diana has a theory that 99% of us feel pretty inadequate quite a lot of the time: our upbringing has instilled the belief that we're not important. And things don't improve when we grow up. We're still inclined to walk into a room full of people feeling two inches tall, imagining that everyone else feels their full height, and this can be pretty intimidating.

So, just supposing that picking up the telephone to make a call, going to a meeting with strangers, making a presentation, or any other situation you care to think of, scares the daylights out of you, we have a question for you. *How do you know it's fear?*

- What do you see, hear, feel, taste and/or smell that tells you that it is fear?
- Is it a horrible picture in your mind's eye?
- Is it an alarming voice in your mind's ear? Or another horrible sound?
- Is it a dreadful feeling?
- Is it a nasty taste or smell?
- Or is it something completely different?

Something's happening inside you that you have interpreted as fear; but what you are getting is a message from your unconscious mind (which wants nothing but the best for you) to which you need to pay attention – otherwise it will just get worse!

So, if it's a picture in your mind's eye, move it far enough away from you so that you can still see it, but it's not frightening any more; if it's a sound in your mind's ear, turn the volume down so that you can still hear it, but it's not frightening; if it's a feeling, let it float out of the window and stretch and fly in the fresh air.

Whatever it is, it's on your side, but it's not communicating very effectively – so ask it what it wants for you. The answer will surprise you; you'll discover that you have a most powerful ally – Your Self – so huge thanks are in order. (However weird this may seem, try it. It works.)

And now comes negotiation time. How can this valuable part of you get its message across to you in a way that you will understand, and respond to? In other words, supposing it wants you to relax, and enjoy the situation, what pictures do you want it to show you in your mind's eye? What would you like to hear in your mind's ear (if it's words, what tone of voice would you like?)? How would you like to feel? How much saliva would you like to have in your mouth, and what lovely smell would you like to have in your nostrils to make you relax and enjoy the situation? Your unconscious mind is yours, and it will do anything you ask, because it has nothing but your best interests at heart.

And while you're about it, how about a profuse apology for misinterpreting its positive intentions?

Dealing with intimidating people

We all know people who find some other people difficult to cope with, and in a hierarchical company, there may be several people each trying to protect their own corners in the best way they know how. For some people, the best form of defence is attack. Here is a useful trick for dealing with difficult people; it was developed by Robert Dilts and the late Todd Epstein of the NLP University, from the Perceptual Positions exercise you did earlier (which was created by Richard Bandler and John Grinder, co-founders of NLP). It's called The Meta-Mirror – and it's also brilliant for mothers-in-law.

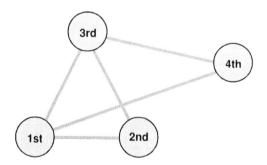

Fig 6.1 – The Meta-Mirror

Think about somebody you have problems with – maybe he or she gives you a hard time, maybe you feel that you cannot communicate with each other, maybe you have just had a fearful row (let's call that person 'X').

Then stand, as yourself, in 1st Position and imagine that X is standing in front of you. What are you experiencing in this position, looking at X?

- What sort of pictures are you seeing in your mind's eye?
- What sort of sounds are you hearing in your mind's ear?
- What sort of feelings are you experiencing, and where are you experiencing them?

For example, what has happened to your breathing, your heart rate, the level of saliva in your mouth? What is going on in your stomach? And so on.

When you have spent enough time in 1st Position to be aware of what is going on, shake all that nastiness off and leave it there.

Then you can step into X's shoes, into 2nd Position, and just stand there, being X. What do you experience in that position? What is going on inside X in 2nd Position? Describe what you experience *as though you were X*, standing in front of you, by saying ...

'I see ... ... I hear ... ... I feel ... ...'

... and describe what you observe, as X, about that you in 1st position: talk about yourself (that person you are now looking at) by name. When you have discovered what is going on inside X (and you'll be surprised how much information you get), shake everything off, leave it there and step out of 2nd position.

Now step into 3rd Position (see diagram), as far away from 1st and 2nd as you need to be in order to be able to observe what is going on between those two people over there. You are now the detached observer, so fold your arms, and lean back a bit, to get yourself into 'detached observer' mode. Describe what is going on between that you over there and X, referring to yourself by name.

- What is that 'you' doing?
- What is X doing?
- How would you describe the interaction between those two people? Defensive? Aggressive? Passive? Uneasy? Or something completely different?

When you have taken in all the information that you need, step out of 3rd Position, and choose a 4th Position, where you can be right outside and observe the relationship between the 'you' in 1st Position, and the 'you' in 3rd Position.

- Are those two 'yous' the same age?
- Are they the same size?
- Is one wiser than the other?
- Is one more vulnerable than the other?
- What do they think of each other?

You will discover that each of those 'yous' has qualities that the other needs, and you will become aware that the 'you' in 1st Position is probably not the person who is fully able to cope with this situation.

Then you can ask yourself whether the 'you' in 3rd Position would be a better person to deal with X. If the answer is 'yes', collect the 'you' in 3rd Position and take that 'you' back to 1st position, (putting the more vulnerable 'you' in a very safe place). Now look at X again, and become aware how everything has changed.

When you have fully appreciated how the change in yourself has affected the situation, you can move into 2nd Position, where you will discover that everything has changed for X as well. As X, you will discover that this other 'you' cannot be treated in the same way; this other 'you' requires respect.

When you have fully appreciated just how much X has changed as well, shake X off, and step back into 1st Position, be who you really are, and enjoy it all over again.

(You may find that you would prefer to move from 4th Position, out into a 5th Position which is even more detached – maybe standing on a chair to give yourself an overview of the situation – and that the 'you' in 4th Position is the person who needs to be in 1st. If so, you can do exactly the same swap with the 'you' in 4th Position.)

When Diana first read this exercise in one of Robert Dilts's books, she thought 'how weird!' It wasn't until she saw it done that she realised how powerful it was.

Cultural fear

Cultural individual, or cultural collective, fear is established over a prolonged period of time due to the input of one-sided information. Here are some examples:

- A person or company may not introduce a new product for fear of making mistakes.
- A country may not join the Single European Currency, for fear of losing its sovereignty.
- A person or nation may fear breaking the rules or the law, for fear of loss of social standing, or of anarchy.
- A person or nation may fear to interact with others because of historical enmity.
- Many people, or companies in a recession, fear creative decisions and actions.
- Many people fear taking even calculated risks.

● Fear of change: this seems to be pretty universal. The phrase 'better the devil you know than the devil you don't' has its equivalents in both French and German, and Spanish is even more interesting – it talks about the bad you know being better than the good you don't.

How many times have we heard: *'The British stick to their traditions'; 'The Germans stick to their rules'; 'The French will only buy French'; 'The Americans only understand the USA'; 'We'd better not buy this company as their products are not yet fully proven'; 'Why should we change tactics? Let's cut costs'?* These cultural collective fears undermine international business, and are more powerful than we sometimes anticipate.

Let's examine and translate these to CAT.

● 'We are better than the rest of the world' syndrome
● Fear of losing control and power to outsiders
● One-sided or biased information (e.g. media, government, education, religion etc)

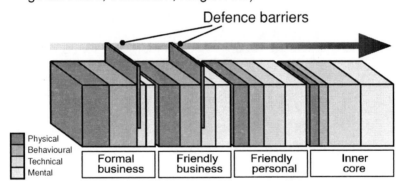

Fig 6.2 – Cultural Fears

Figure 6.2 shows two defence barriers: one in the formal business aura, between the behavioural and the technical sub-aura, and a second in the friendly business aura between the same sub-auras. In other words, if we disregard the physical and behavioural objections, we will still be confronted with underlying cultural disinformation – in other words, powerful belief-level fears.

As we saw in the chapter: 'The Cultural Auras Theory', the technical aura is very much influenced by what's going on at the moment, and these fears can also be due to whatever evolutionary process a person, a company or a nation is undergoing: people are having to come out of their comfort zones, and may feel themselves on unstable ground.

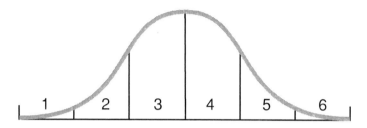

Phase 1 - Exploratory
Phase 2 - Exponential growth
Phase 3 - Slowing growth
Phase 4 - Slow decline
Phase 5 - Fast decline
Phase 6 - Death

Fig 6.3 – The different phases in an evolutionary process.

Figure 6.3 shows the different phases of any evolutionary process:

1. In the exploratory phase, once we have decided to go for it, there is no fear. We try whatever is possible to achieve our goals, whether this be the creation of a new product, or the marketing of a new product: we're like children learning to walk – it's exciting, and there's no space for doubts.
2. In the second phase, growth is exponential – thanks to our initial success – so we're quite happy.
3. In phase 3, we're still growing, but not so fast; and this is where we start to experience a different mind-set. Our initial efforts have made us successful, and we have become used to this 'traditional' way of achieving our goals. At this point most of us start to fear changing the initial method, as we have known this to be successful – so we go on doing what we've always done, despite all the signals that this might not necessarily be sensible.
4. In this phase we have slowly, grindingly reached the peak, and the only way from here is down.
5. The decline phase that inevitably follows is the result of our fear in

phase 3 to re-address our initial method, and adapt or change this according to the overall evolution around us.

6. Death follows and that is the only thing we can predict with 100% certainty.

We do not need much imagination to understand that this pattern illustrates the decline and fall of many nations, companies and even individuals.

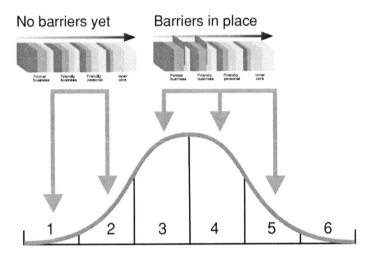

Fig 6.4 – Defence barriers created as a result of evolutionary tradition

Figure 6.4 shows us what happens when we apply CAT to this scenario. In phases 1 and 2, all the thought and energy flows freely into the new project; but, from phase 3 onwards, the defence barriers are in place and the information that matters can't get in or out.

To discover where people are in this evolutionary phase, all we need to do is listen to what they say:

- *Why should we change our process/product?* (We have been making money)
- *Why should we change our thinking process?* (It brought us a long way)
- *We're not making any profit any longer, so let's cut costs.*
- *Let's introduce some guidelines/directives/laws to enable us to increase our control.*

Fear is the most powerful reason for sabotaging ourselves; and sometimes it is so deeply ingrained that we are not aware of what we are doing (as Sir Humphrey, in +, would have it: *'It's been done this way for two hundred years: therefore it must be right'*. As head of the Civil Service, Sir Humphrey would not tolerate change: it would upset his carefully ordered life). Fear has the same effect on individuals, groups, companies and nations. There are numerous examples in history – the downfall of many empires, the downfall of the car industry in the UK, the downfall of international corporations, and so on.

How can we assuage these fears?

It is practically impossible to by-pass a collective cultural fear if we are dealing with a nation; but, in international business, we are seldom confronted with this problem. Usually we are dealing with a company, or rather individuals representing a company or an institute. So let's start by thinking what may be going on inside these poor, fearful people.

Remember Diana's theory that 99% of us feel pretty inadequate quite a lot of the time – this means that most of us feel at some disadvantage quite frequently. So, people are feeling vulnerable, and needing to protect themselves; and here you are proposing CHANGE!

> **Try an experiment:**
>
> Clasp your hands together in the way that you normally do, and notice which hand or which thumb is on top. If you've interlocked your fingers, is your right index finger on top, or your left?
>
> Now clasp them together in the opposite way. What happens? What does it feel like?
>
> People say it feels weird, strange, uncomfortable and so on, and they want to change back. It's different. But the question we would ask you is: is it dangerous?

All too often, we come across something that is different, and we feel uncomfortable; so, instead of asking ourselves why we feel so uncomfortable, we instantly decide that, if we feel that way, it must be dangerous, and therefore must be avoided. All that is really happening is that our unconscious mind is sending us a message that we need to notice that something is different. This comes under the Dangerous Art of Mind Reading – and this time it is our own minds.

Once we realise that our proposition may have generated thoughts of CHANGE! in the other person's mind, and that CHANGE! feels so uncomfortable, that they're not prepared even to think about it, we know what we are dealing with. And the trick here is to join the other person in their model of the world: understand and appreciate what they are experiencing, and talk them through it stage by stage.

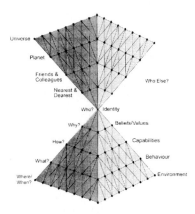

Another useful tool is the Logical Levels Chart that we have seen before – here it is again as a reminder. We need to ask ourselves at what Logical Level this fear is perceived.

If we're just suggesting a change in behaviour, and that seems to present difficulties, we can go up to capability level: have they got, or can they get, the wherewithal to take this on? If necessary, we can then go up to beliefs/values level: if they can provide the wherewithal, do they believe they can do it? Do they believe it would be worthwhile? Does it fit in with their values and/or the company's values?

If we've done our homework, and studied the culture, we are unlikely to be bringing in a proposal that threatens their beliefs and values – which would make their identity feel a bit shaky. But, should something unforeseen occur, we would need to move up to identity level or above, to assuage any of these fears.

If our proposal threatens who they are, there is no way it will work, unless we go up to a yet higher level, and can demonstrate that their identity will be enhanced within the system they are in. As we saw in the last chapter, hierarchy is a great fear-creator; so, if this is the kind of company we find ourselves in, an identity-level change may seem impossibly threatening. Maybe they can foresee our taking over the project, or bringing someone else in to run it, which would result in their losing status within their company. Whatever they perceive is real to them, so we need to be very aware of what the issues might be.

If our proposal threatens their nearest and dearest, or their company or anything else that belongs to them, we could find ourselves in serious trouble! If they might lose their jobs, how would they feed their families? If it threatens the future of the company, not only are their jobs at stake, but also the jobs of all their colleagues, and the honour of the company.

On the subject of change, a colleague of Diana's was called in urgently because someone, whom we shall call Pete, was driving all his colleagues mad with his new ideas about Quality Control, and they couldn't take any more. Nelda is a brilliant NLP-er and, the moment Pete announced that Quality Control was his new religion, she realised that the level he was coming from was far too high for comfort; so she smiled up at him sweetly, and asked: 'does that mean you're prepared to die for it?' There was a long silence as Pete realised that he needed to bring Quality Control down from planet level to belief level, where it belonged. And peace was restored.

Some thoughts on values

The Brahma Kumaris, an extraordinary world-wide organisation, did a survey of values around the world, from which they discovered that – no matter what race, colour or creed we may be – we all share the top nine values. In conjunction with the United Nations, they have put together a whole series of educational programmes for schools and colleges. The schools that are using them not only have few behavioural problems, but also have excellent exam results. The values they study are, in no particular order: **peace, respect, love, responsibility, happiness, tolerance, co-operation, honesty, humility, simplicity** and **unity**. (See Living Values in the bibliography.)

As a result of this research, we know that anywhere we go in the world, if we honour these values, we'll be able to create the relationships we need, to do effective business.

Suppose you are feeling nervous about a particular meeting, for whatever reason, we now have an interesting experiment for you.

Take your time, it will be worth it.

- ⊛ Think about something you really enjoy doing; and then think about something you hate doing.

- ⊛ Then switch your thoughts back and forth from one situation to the other, and notice how different you feel in the two situations; for example, do you feel light or heavy, warm, cool or cold? Do you feel stillness or movement inside you? Do your muscles feel tight or relaxed? What else do you notice about how you feel?

- ⊛ Now look at the pictures in your mind's eye, in the different situations: are they in black and white or in colour? Are they still or moving? Are you living the pictures, or are you watching yourself? What other differences do you notice?

- ⊛ Now listen to the sounds in your mind's ear. Is there chatter or noise going on? If there is chatter, whose voice is it? Or is all quiet inside your head? What else is different as you listen to the sounds in your mind's ear?

- ⊛ How much saliva have you got in your mouth on each occasion? And do you notice any other tastes or smells in the different situations?

- ⊛ And, most importantly, how big is the safe space around you when you're doing something you love, compared to something you hate?

- ⊛ And now, comparing the two situations, be aware of the differences in the safe space you have around you as you experience something you love doing, and something you hate doing. For example, have you got room to think and to manoeuvre when you're doing what you love? Have you got room to think in the situation you hate? How big is the space when you're doing something you love? And how big is it when you're doing something that you hate?

As you will have discovered, what you experience in those two opposing situations is completely different. And what is even more interesting, is that you made them both up – just to oblige us.

So you have just proved to yourself that you can make anything up. The main discovery, from the above exercise, is the huge safe space you created around you, when you were thinking about something you love doing. Experiment with making that space even bigger. What happens?

The two important things about this space are:

1. You made it up, just to oblige us, so you can make it up whenever you want. Or you can just install it now, and take it everywhere you go.
2. It's yours. So, just as if you were inviting someone into your house, you invite people into it; and, because it is safe, the people who come into it feel safe too. Just as you wouldn't behave badly in someone else's house, you'll find that people behave beautifully in your space.

If we think about being 'under pressure': we realise that this is what happens when we've allowed our safe space to get so small that we've got no room to think, or to manoeuvre: the outside world is pressing down on us. But, now that you have discovered what goes on, you can be aware the moment your space starts shrinking, and immediately expand it again – just like you did a few minutes ago.

If you think all this is barking mad, you owe it to your scepticism to try it out. Take your safe space and play with it: try it with your friends and see what happens, try it out with perfect strangers, and see how many interesting new people you meet; and, once you are used to it and enjoying it, try it out in difficult situations, and see what changes.

While you're about it: what would happen if you took your big, safe space into the situation you were experimenting with earlier – the one you hate? What difference would it make? Then imagine taking it to that meeting you were nervous about – notice how much more comfortable you feel, and how differently the other person/people respond to you because you are feeling good.

We all need to feel safe

Of our three brains, the oldest is the reptilian brain, or brain stem. It is responsible for territory, and for fight or flight. Its job is to keep us safe, and it is this brain that puts up the barriers to ensure our protection.

So, now that we have discovered how to keep ourselves safe, by creating our own space, we can use this to make the other person feel safe too. All we need to do is take our big, safe space with us, invite other people into it and, as we talk and listen to them, think: 'this person really matters to me', and the relationship is already established, in the heart, at identity level.

Here is another experiment (you'll need to find someone to do it with):

Find something you disagree about (this is the difficult bit. Politics and religion are generally good sources of argument). And discuss this topic for a few minutes, in each of the following positions.

1. Face to face, sitting down

2. Back to back sitting down

3. Side by side, sitting down

4. Face to face, standing up

5. Back to back, standing up

6. Side by side, standing up

7. Side by side, walking along

What happens? Which is the easiest way of discussing things, and why? And which is the most difficult, and why? Does your partner agree with your findings? Or does he or she prefer to do things differently?

And, while we're on the subject of feeling safe, and disagreement, here is another experiment (this time you'll need two people):

Get one person to hold out an arm to the side, at right angles to his or her body. Say you are going to test his strength by pushing down gently on his wrist bone, and ask him to resist. When you do this, you will find he is quite strong.

Now get the third person to point a finger at the person you are testing, and look him or her straight in the eye. You will find that suddenly the arm strength is gone.

And the moral of this experiment? Pointing a finger at someone is seriously deleterious.

On telling the truth

As we have seen in earlier chapters, trust and relationship are all-important in most cultures, when it comes to business. To this end, there is nothing like the power of the truth: of laying our business cards on the table. If we are up front about any problems we may have, they may have the solution; but, if they discover later that we didn't admit to a problem, that will be the end of our business, and our reputation in that country will be worthless.

(Incidentally, never take the Iranians on at their version of liar dice: they'll know when you're lying and you won't know when they are. It's all to do with a vein that throbs the moment you stray from the truth.)

Converting fear into enthusiasm

So, we've identified the fear, and discussed and appreciated the position our new friend is in (for simplicity, we're going to imagine he's a man). We can now work with the fear, and convert it into enthusiasm. To do this, we need to remember that we have no answers (it's not our business we're talking about, it's his); what we do have is a series of very good questions.

- *How do you see the future of your company?* We want to know if they think they'll survive without making any changes, but we're not going to ask, or

- *Do you see a need to change your process/product(s) and procedures, in the changing environment you're operating in?*

- *How will you adapt your process/product(s) and procedures in the changing environment you're operating in?*

- *How will you stay competitive in this environment?*

- *How can we help you to stay competitive?*

We may well find that he has all the answers; but, with his hands tied behind his back by the company hierarchy, you may not get very far. Now that you know where you are, remember that this company took a long time to get to this stage, so it may take a long time to help them change their minds. Commercial arguments are usually wasted: find the key decision makers, and repeat the above until you have the confidence to move to step 2: The Negotiation (see Chapter 10).

Reasons for losing business:

- running out of time
- failure to understand the underlying fear
- not being persistent enough.

And, incidentally, these reasons also apply to marriages, teamwork and politics. Be persistent about achieving your goals and success is yours.

Some thoughts on racism

Foreigners are different! And it is this very difference that can make people feel uncomfortable at an unconscious level – just like clasping our hands together the 'wrong' way. If we go back to the 'fight or flight' concept, we realise that some people, when they feel unsafe, become aggressive, whereas other avoid the supposed threat like the plague. The trick, as always, is to be aware of what is going on in our thinking process.

F*** Word Checklist

1. Do your homework, and get an understanding of the new culture.

2. Take your big safe space into the meeting with you.

3. Remember that a fearful person may not look reassuring at first sight, and make allowances.

4. Welcome the new colleague into your safe space.

5. Show respect at all time, and make him/her feel important: this person really matters to you.

6. Sit side by side, rather than face to face.

7. Maybe some small talk would be useful and reassuring - go with the flow.

8. Be aware of how much reassuring small talk this person may need (in some countries, this may take several meetings).

9. Introduce your proposal by placing it on the table, in front of you, to ensure that you're 'on the same side', and engage his/her interest.

10. Explain your product/service/company simply and clearly.

11. Listen, carefully, to the responses.

12. Analyse the responses, to ensure that you have been clearly understood; if in doubt, explain in different way.

13. Keep focussing on the new colleague's technical abilities.

14. Allow him or her to interrupt at any time, and place all interruptions in context.

14. Identify the logical levels of any and all constraints resulting from cultural fear.

16. Remember that all fear is valid, even if it seems ridiculous to you: respect it and work with it.

17. Explain the possibilities of doing business, in view of these fears.

18. Run these possibilities into the future, to allay the fears at every level.

19. Convert the fear into enthusiasm.

20. Analyse what has been said, and repeat questions, if need be.

21. Now that you have a feel for the other person's business approach, consult him/her about how to pursue the business.

Before we move on, it's time to review our 10 Steps to Success. We have added fear to No 4.

The 10 steps

1. Analyse the area/country to visit prior to the trip.

2. Get some understanding of its history/culture.

3. Possibly learn some of the language.

4. Understand as much of their paradigms and fears as possible.

5. Apply CAT with the person(s) you are meeting.

6. Repeat until you feel confident about the relationship.

7.   Always analyse what went right and what wrong.

8.   Always ask your host(s) to summarise how they see the process evolving.

9.   Always be open-minded to new influences.

10. Never stick to one paradigm.

7

Bloody Foreigners!
I: The Europeans

This chapter gives you some background information on different cultures to set the scene, and a light-hearted collection of observations from travels around the world, to give you a flavour of some of the situations you might find yourself in, in assorted countries. They are entirely subjective observations, and you may find that things turn out quite differently. We also give you some guidance on which Auras are the most appropriate in which to do business in the different cultures.

Many nations were and are established from influxes of outside cultures. For example, in the last century, a mass of Germans, Iranians, Afghans, Russians, Poles, Hungarians, Moroccans, Turks, and many more, left their home countries and migrated to other parts of the world, bringing with them their own cultures, and creating changes in some local traditions.

One of the most striking examples is of course the USA, which is made up of a whole range of different cultures that went into the melting-pot; and now – whether they were originally natives or immigrants – all these people consider themselves US citizens. This is in direct opposition to the Europeans who are made up of a collection of different nations, each with its own culture, and each speaking its own language.

Europe

Europe has, down the ages, had invasions from within and without its borders. The Celts, Romans, Franks, Normans, French, Spanish, Dutch and Germans amongst others have all tried to annex their neighbours, while the Ottomans and several other Asian communities have tried to conquer Europe from the outside. European nations have been fighting one another for over two millennia, and the European Union created in the last century by no means makes Europe one happy family. It certainly makes business simpler within the community, but the diversity of cultures will remain for generations to come – unlike the USA where they consider themselves all one race.

From the business point of view, we can divide Europe into two parts: the more law-abiding Protestant or related religions, in the North, and the more relaxed Catholic, or notoriously corrupt, region in the South. So what's religion got to do with anything? Religion not only operates at belief level, it is also something we belong to – so it comes very high up in the logical levels of thinking.

The Nordic countries (Scandinavia, Finland, Germany, the UK and the Netherlands) show some similar traits. These countries were far enough away from Rome, and the Pope, to be able to reform their churches; and those in charge of these reforms took life pretty seriously.

The British

If Ron were to write a book about the Brits, it would be called *Temporarily Unavailable*, because of the supermarket signs, relating to many of the products one might want to buy. They are 'awfully sorry' about this and they have no idea when they will be available. Ron states flatly that the concept of service in England is a joke, and all Diana can say (weakly) in reply is that service is infinitely better than it was 30 years ago – largely due to immigrants who were prepared to work hard, and keep their businesses open late.

The UK is a great mix of race and religion; but, because it is surrounded by water, it is of an insular turn of mind, and the defence barriers we saw earlier were established long ago. These may not be as pronounced as in some other countries, and building a long-term relationship is essential to success in business here (unlike with their Anglo-Saxon brothers and sisters in the USA). Building this relationship may take longer than anticipated, but be persistent and you will be amply rewarded.

Formality changes rapidly into a certain informality, but do not underestimate the Brits: they like to be classy. Their language leaves a lot unsaid, and they appreciate people with a sense of humour.

Presentations to groups of people are usually quite formal, and interaction with the speaker is limited – but you need humour to keep the audience awake.

Normally, one doesn't interrupt another person during a conversation, and when A has finished speaking, B will continue immediately; there is no pause for consideration of what has been said, as there would be in Japan.

Decisions are not made as swiftly as in the USA, and may take years – especially if one is introducing a new product which has not been tried and tested according to 700 years of tradition.

As islanders, the Brits have had little interaction with other cultures, although when one wanders round London, one feels as if one is surrounded by every nationality one can think of – but, at the end of the day, these people are all bloody foreigners.

The perception of business in the UK is totally different from many other nations, and foreigners could be forgiven for thinking that the Brits will never get to the point. From all Ron's business meetings in the UK, he can count on one hand the times where they went straight to the point. Usually there is some talk about the government, which by definition is always wrong, followed by how the industry is doing and the latest gossip. Imagine that you are at the theatre and you will realise that business in the UK is not done until the fourth or the fifth act.

An American friend of Ron's, who is in the UK on assignment for a major US company, told him how they had failed to get any deals with UK companies: *'We made them offers. We gave presentation after presentation. We had our technical people fly in from the USA. We compiled technical reports. We had our lawyers review the contracts on offer. They even told us that they approved of our product and service. Nonetheless we lost, time and again.'*

After reading the draft script of this book, he said: *'It is now clear to me that we had forgotten the essential bit: building up a relationship with the key figures involved, and not talking business from the word 'go', like we do in the USA.'* He added that it also explained why they had experienced similar problems in other parts of Europe.

The Brits need to build up a good relationship, especially with foreigners, before they commit. It takes time – and sometimes a lot more than one would anticipate. For example, the first time around, they may tell you that they are very interested in the deal, product or service, or that they will definitely consider it, or that it's better than anything they have seen so far, and so on. Don't be fooled – they need to buy time and get to know you better.

The one thing the Brits have in great amounts is humour – in which irony and understatement play a big part: understanding their humour is a tremendous asset, as it can be used to break the ice.

Get yourself into the Friendly Business Aura or, even better, Friendly Personal before you even contemplate discussing business.

To return to *Temporarily Unavailable*: one thing you need to know if, for instance, you want to buy a UK company or start a Joint Venture, is that the urge to please customers is seriously lacking in the UK – although there are, of course, notable exceptions to this rule.

A lot of business in the UK is left to youngsters, aged from 16 upwards. These youngsters are in charge of serving customers in shops, and often as committed to their jobs as turkeys are to Christmas. The one ambition in life of many waiters and waitresses in restaurants throughout the UK is to plan their next Saturday night out. The companies save lots of money by employing these nice, cheap people. As a customer, you can ask for the simplest thing in a shop, and the assistants may look at you as if you come from another planet. Upset the customers and they won't come back: these companies have no idea of how much money they are losing, relative to what they are saving.

> When the Roets arrived in England, they decided to buy a television and a satellite dish so that their children (who spoke no English at that stage) could still watch one of the Dutch channels.
>
> Two engineers came to install the dish. They looked at the walls of the house, which were (like all old Cotswold houses) 2 feet deep, sucked their teeth, and came to the conclusion that they did not have the right drill bit. Fair enough, a new appointment was made.
>
> Two days later another pair of engineers came round; they too looked at the walls, sucked their teeth, and concluded that they did not have the right bit.
>
> Seven phone calls and 45 minutes later, Ron extracted the promise: 'tomorrow, Saturday, an engineer will come to your house with the correct tools.' And, indeed up the engineer turned, looked at the walls and concluded that he didn't have the right bit. Was this a practical joke? Ron enquired. It wasn't. So Ron hired a drill and did the job himself.

The Brits just don't seem to have grasped that, without customers, you have no business.

Another element of the UK, which can drive foreigners ballistic, is the red tape. Rules must be obeyed even if this means that business is put on hold, and this frequently gets beyond a joke. While the rule culture is found in most Protestant countries throughout Europe, the British version can drive even the easy-going Danes mad.

The chameleon thrives in Britain because it blends effortlessly into the background. According to Diana's grandmother, almost the worst thing you could say about anybody was that they were 'noticeable'. People who drew attention to themselves were beyond the pale, and there was only one crime worse than being noticeable, and that was to be 'most noticeable'. The Brits like people who fit in.

For a closer understanding of the Brits, you'll enjoy *Yes, Minister*, and *Yes, Prime Minister* by Jonathan Lynn and Anthony Jay, and also George Mikes's (pronounced Meekesh) *How to be an Alien* (see bibliography).

The Germans

The Germans have their defence barriers, which are called 'the rules'. *'Ordnung muss sein'* – there must be order. Their belief is that, without order, chaos will inevitably ensue: no mowing on Sunday, no car washing on Sunday, garden bonfires only allowed on certain days (so you know when you can hang out your washing), and so on. They are also extremely safety-conscious.

Business in Germany, in contrast to the UK, is not a laughing matter. It has to be formal and correct – not emotional like the Southern parts of Europe – and according to all the rules. We don't introduce ourselves by our first names, and we address Dr Schwartz as Herr Doktor. The Germans are excellent linguists and, in some companies, staff meetings are conducted in English.

Like the Dutch, the Germans can come across as blunt, because they don't beat about the bush. On the whole, they have been pretty good at international business over many centuries, and have lately come to understand that Germany is only a cog in the worldwide business machinery.

Depending on the nature of your business, and especially when it is longer term, a sound relationship is necessary. Like the UK, it is better to move to the Friendly Personal Aura, but you can easily do business longer term in the Friendly Business Aura in contrast to the UK.

The Dutch

The Dutch know it all and will tell the world how to wheel and deal.

Although, primarily, they have trade in their blood, and no defence barriers, you might occasionally come across a defensive, insular Dutchman.

A spade is a spade – they don't mess about, and they don't joke about spades. But they do enjoy subtle humour.

The Dutch were a very affluent maritime nation, and trading was and is high on their agenda. They are sincere business people: 'Yes' means 'Yes', and 'No' means 'don't come back'. During the Shogun era in Japan, there were only two nations allowed to trade with the isolated Japanese and these were the Dutch and the Portuguese. No other nation worldwide was so successful at trading.

Because the Dutch like to show the rest of the world how to do things, drugs are readily available in the Netherlands. This is so typical! None of the other European countries has similar ideas. Consequently, the drug traffic between the Netherlands and the rest of Europe is ever increasing. It is like playing football with different rules from the rest of the world.

> Remembering that Ron is Dutch, here's a typical know-it-all story: he was off to Helsinki in the middle of winter and his wife, Monique, suggested that he get himself a hat. What rubbish! Who was the traveller in the family? What could she possibly know?
>
> Strolling round the city, in a temperature of -30° Centigrade, (very, very cold for Fahrenheit readers) he wondered why so many people were wearing fur hats; and, on returning to his hotel, he discovered that his ears were the colour of beetroot, and becoming very painful as they thawed out.

Another example of possibly carrying knowing best a bit too far: in July a serious exodus of thousands and thousands of caravans and mobile homes fills up the *Route du Soleil* on their way to France's *Côte d'Azur*. For the Dutch, foreign French food is beyond the pale, so they take all their food with them. The French had a humour failure when they discovered two Dutch caravans turned into grocery shops, and selling only Dutch produce on the camping sites.

Call it conservatism or plain bloody stubbornness, most Dutch people need strong evidence before they will contemplate taking a new idea on board; but, once they have accepted our idea, we can have some of the best possible business relationships with our Dutch colleagues. We can make deals in Friendly Business, as it may take a real effort to get into Friendly Personal.

The Belgians

Belgium, in the centre of Europe, is a fairly new country and only became independent in 1830. There are no Belgians: the population consists of Flemish, Walloons, a minority of German speakers and an awkward mixture of Flemish and Walloons living in Brussels.

Belgium has been invaded and ruled by more nations than most other European countries, and its history has created pronounced defence barriers – particularly when doing business, and to a lesser extent when trading with foreigners.

At the time it became independent, the Walloons, the French-speaking citizens, were the ruling class. Lawyers, doctors and other professionals spoke French. The Flemish were the labourers, farmers and so on. It was not until the major riots in the 1960s that this changed. The Walloon part of the country was then the powerhouse of the country, with its heavy industry and coal mines responsible for the lion's share of the GNP. Today it is the Flemish part, and especially the province of West Flanders, which is the powerhouse of the country.

The game in Belgium is: 'How to avoid the law and particularly any tax law', and the University of Leuven published a paper in the 1990s demonstrating that the Belgian government was more corrupt than the Mafia in Italy. So do not expect the Belgians to be straightforward.

This small country has many diverse attitudes towards business: for example, in Limburg, a province in the North, business is tough as trust is not the name of the game; whereas, in the province of West Flanders, the Silicon Valley of Belgium, trust and relationship building is exactly what business is all about.

There is a lot of innuendo in Belgian business, both in their language and in their overall attitudes. Business is not exactly a laughing matter and, once they understand the financial benefits, it can go smoothly.

It can take some doing to get to the Friendly Personal Aura but, once there, business is as easy as falling off a log. Trust is the name of the game, although this takes more time to achieve than in any neighbouring country – and we need to remember that this is only because of their history.

The French

The French, like the Dutch, know it all. But, rather than telling the world, they keep it to themselves and anything French is by definition good, whereas anything foreign is second class. The French still have ideas of empire, and do not like to be ruled.

While they have a tendency, like the Germans, to consider business as a serious matter, they can also be pretty relaxed and a decision may mean anything from 'Yes' to 'No' (a typical Latin trait). They may give the impression that their decisions depend on which way the wind is blowing, and then they can change them at will.

If we want to be successful in France, we need to establish a French subsidiary, or at least give the product to be sold a typical French name.

The French, in Formal Business, are a serious bunch: humour is not used, as this might come over as a lack of sincerity. However, once the ice has melted they can be fun to work with. The melting may take some time, unless the other party speaks French – so we would suggest that you learn at least some of the language.

The French are hierarchical and one needs to be aware that the correct titles are used. At staff meetings, the seating is arranged according to rank.

Once again, relationship is the key. Business can be conducted in the Friendly Business Aura and, over time, one might get into Friendly Personal – although it isn't easy as a foreigner, unless one has been introduced by another French person when suddenly you find yourself a part of their culture.

Rumour has it that the French are arrogant, and won't speak anything but French. Not so. The reason they prefer you to speak French is because they are terrified of making fools of themselves in English. When Diana was living in Berlin, she had about 60 students learning English – all paid for by the French Government; whereas, apart from the Intelligence Company, she had one English student learning French. They also send their children across to England in droves during school holidays.

Diana's bible, when she lived in France was Pierre Daninos's *Les Carnets du Major Thompson* (see bibliography). This book describes life in France through the eyes of a retired British Army officer, married to a French woman. It is wonderfully funny and extremely accurate. The interesting thing about this book is that the French find it hysterically funny about the English, and the English find it hysterically funny about the French. Neither nation thinks it remotely funny about themselves. The English version is called *Major Thompson's Diaries* which, at the time of writing, sad to say, is out of print.

The Irish

The Irish are a fun crowd, they have this *'je ne sais quoi'*, and they are very friendly to do business with. Once yours, they are forever yours, although it takes a lot of Guinness and persuasion before they commit. It may take ages before they decide, and even then they have the most wonderful excuses why they can't do it yet.

The Irish consider the English as Big Brother. They do not mind foreigners and have no problem with the Dutch, even though the Protestants in the North still grow Sweet Williams and orange lilies, just to annoy the Catholics by reminding them of the Dutch Willem van Oranje (William of Orange) who became King of England. Time, as in the Latin countries, is very flexible. There are 24 hours in a day and that is all one needs to know.

Driving in the Republic of Ireland is an exhilarating experience. The roads were designed and constructed for horse-drawn carts, rather than modern automobiles. Consequently one finds many cars parked in ditches and fields, as the roads surprise even the inhabitants.

The best advice for doing business with Irish is to learn everything about organised chaos. Their 'Yes' may mean anything under the sun. Watching paint dry takes less time than waiting for the Irish to make a decision.

Once you do business with them you are friends for life; and don't be fooled by their enormous friendliness – they are shrewd business people.

Forget the business auras: build up a relationship in Friendly Personal.

The Italians

Going to Italy is an adventure in itself. Avoid all Italian airlines and, if you have no choice, take an early morning flight so that, with luck, you'll arrive in time for dinner. Otherwise, your first impression of Italy will be one of inefficiency.

The wonderful thing about the Italians is their elegance. They dress like no other nation. The words that spring to mind are: chic, daring, sexy but elegant and magnificent. Not only do they dress well but everything they produce, like magazines, household products, equipment, furniture and so on has a certain charm, and is pleasing to the eye.

Business is conducted in style and about style.

Italians need to talk.

When the taxi-driver collecting you from the airport at Rome or Milan realises that you do not speak Italian, and that he'll have no one to talk to, he picks up his mobile phone and starts calling all his friends instead – whilst driving in the most chaotic traffic in the world, apart maybe from Bangkok and Tehran.

The Italians have this insatiable urge to express themselves both verbally and physically. They are masters of the art of bargaining, like many other Mediterranean and Asian nations.

Time in Italy is incredibly flexible. Unlike Germany, where an appointment at 10 o'clock means 10 o'clock and not five past, or the deal is lost, in Italy and most Latin countries the appointment may be at any time between 9.45 and 10.30. In the Arab world it is even more flexible and one is lucky to see the person in question on the day the appointment was fixed. The Italians are great networkers, preferably within their own business community. They have time for foreigners, but the outsider needs to appreciate that business will be concluded only after a certain period of time, as it is often secondary to the many other things they are involved in.

In a business conversation they may interrupt when they feel like it. Just get used to this and keep your cool, and your ability to remember where you left off.

Long-term business is always conducted in the Friendly Personal Aura and this will take some time to get into, but not as long as with the Belgians or French.

The Spaniards

The Spaniards are a proud nation and, like the Italians, they are very elegant. They are punctilious when it comes to business, unlike their neighbours across the Mediterranean. To describe them as the '*mañana*' people is out of date.

As in so many European countries, doing business in Spain depends on the relationship.

It is essential for them to get to know you. If they don't, they may take you for a ride. Like other Latins, they prefer some introductory chat before getting down to business. This often happens round the dinner table, and dining doesn't happen before 9.00 pm, because they have had their siestas, and are now enjoying the second half of their day in the cool. Unlike the Italians who come over as very flexible, the Spaniards are a lot more rigid. This may well be because they have been exploited by foreigners in the past.

They did not go to drama school, unlike the Italians, but they use a lot of gestures. Like the Italians, two Spanish businessmen may walk arm in arm – they are not gay, this is a sincere token of appreciation.

Business is considered a serious matter, and we need to ensure that we understand their formalities – for example, no first names until invited.

The Swedes and other Scandinavians

Ron has failed to discover the Swedish sense of humour although he is sure they have one; and he doesn't find doing business with Swedes easy, as the ice does not melt readily.

They have a lot of rules, which they obey without any discussion or debate. For example, in the late 70s and early 80s when drinking and driving was outlawed, each restaurant had its own breathalyser to analyse the content of alcohol. Despite all this, and the exorbitant price of alcohol, one found more drunks in Sweden at that time than in countries where drinking was part of the life style.

Doing business in these countries is pretty straightforward: there are rules, no humour, it's very technical and we need to keep it serious.

Building up a relationship is useful, but not essential; and visiting them a couple of times can work wonders, as they really seem to appreciate it..

Business can be easily conducted in the Friendly Business Aura, because getting to Friendly Personal may take more time than you anticipated. In general, keep it pretty formal; although, in Denmark, you can be more relaxed than in the other countries.

Straight talking is a must just like in the Netherlands and, if you're driving in Sweden, beware of wandering elks: they'll write your car off, and walk away.

The Russians

Although the major part of this vast country lies in Asia, business is primarily done in the European part – at the time of writing. Most Russians think that, in the West, money lies on the pavement to be picked up at one's leisure.

Safety is not the name of the game in Moscow. Doing business over there is a real challenge. One does not know whom one is talking to – they could be key decision makers or just puppets – or whether they are gangsters or honest people. One thing is certain – they need money. Bribery is part of their life style. All in all, it is one of the most challenging places to do business.

On the one hand you will find Russians who made money under the Communist regime and, on the other, serious poverty. Trust is important, but we need to be aware that they don't have much experience of the concept as far as business in concerned. So it will take a fair deal of patience and time to build a good relationship.

The Russians are very sceptical about business as they've been taken for a ride too often. Their defence barriers are understandable and it takes a lot of effort to get through to the Friendly Business Aura, let alone to Friendly Personal. Even if we do get through to Friendly Personal, we must never underestimate their scepticism.

If we give the impression that 'we know best', we will get nowhere; and we always need to remember that they have, and have had, some of the greatest minds in the world.

The Poles and other East Europeans

Ron's experience in Eastern Europe was primarily in the communist days, but he's been back since. The Poles' attitude to business is similar to that of the Russians, in many ways. As we saw earlier, it is important to understand that the communist regime has affected many people's attitudes towards business and to people from the West. When the Wall came down, they had to learn everything about business, and were probably taken for some serious rides. It will take time for them to understand all the aspects of a democratic society. In business it is important to have some knowledge about the past to understand where they are coming from.

The Czechs are pretty hard working and accept Western views more readily than, for instance, the Rumanians.

In contrast to Russia, business can be done in the Friendly Personal Aura especially in Poland, the Czech Republic, Slovakia, Hungary, Bulgaria and some of the former Yugoslavia – but certainly not in Rumania. And we need to remember that Rumania has not had the happiest of histories.

Humour is acceptable: in Communist times it was part of their lifestyle, but nowadays one has to be very careful not to tread on people's toes.

Formality up front is a must. The safest thing is to let them show you the dos and the don'ts.

Success Checklist for Europe

1. Be aware of the history of the country and how it might affect people's thinking.

2. Isolated countries have stronger defence barriers.

3. The Brits are more formal than the Americans and take time to get to the point.

4. The concept of service is a joke in England.

5. Relationship is essential for the Europeans.

6. Be aware of the power of the rules and red tape in some countries.

7. Copy your hosts, as far as formality is concerned.

8. The Dutch call a spade a spade, and do things their way.

9. Be aware of the significance of 'the unsaid' in Europe.

10. Northern and Southern Europeans behave according to their climate, and their distance from Rome.

11. The Iron Curtain affected attitudes to business.

12. Go with the flow: let your hosts dictate the pace.

8

Bloody Foreigners!
II: The Rest of the World

It seems very arrogant to devote a whole chapter to the Europeans and only allot one chapter to the rest of the world; but, as Europeans, Europe is the area we know best, and where we can be most useful to you.

Asia

Asia is an enormous continent encompassing many different nations. We have chosen two countries to discuss: the Japanese for their unique attitudes to business, and the Thais for their exemplary customer service.

The Japanese

When it comes to business, the Japanese decide as a team – rather than as individuals like Americans or Europeans. This decision process can take forever, and one may get the impression that they are not interested in the deal. Have faith!

Never underestimate their knowledge. They are probably the most powerful networkers in the world. Ask a Japanese company to do a market survey and you'll be astonished by what they come up with – they'll find out every detail.

During formal presentations, they will listen quietly. Once again, one may get the impression that they are not interested. Don't be fooled! They will have absorbed more information than anyone else around the table.

They are also extremely polite. During presentations, they will not ask the presenter any questions which they feel might be provocative; there will only be questions to clarify a detail here and there. Only later, in the Sushi bar, will they discuss things at length, in a small committee with the presenter. They might offer their opinions, emphasising that these are personal and not necessarily the company's directive.

The hierarchy in a Japanese company is of the greatest importance, and the outsider needs to be aware of the different ranks and act accordingly. Pay attention to their bowing. Women bow, as well as men; and, the deeper the bow, the more important the person they are bowing to. On arrival, you will be introduced, so you will know how senior the other person is, and be able to respond accordingly. The junior person bows first and, if they are of equal rank, both people bow at the same time, to the same depth. If you are on your first visit, the fact that you bow at all will stand you in excellent stead. Alternatively, take advice on the depth of the bow according to rank, before you go. Either way, you will come across as a well-mannered, highly-educated foreigner – unlike your competitors, and – by copying your equals, will soon get the hang of how to do it properly.

A nice custom, which is catching on in Europe – when you give your business card to a Japanese person, he or she will spend time examining it, and may discuss it, before putting it carefully in a safe place. Taking someone's card and putting it straight in your pocket is considered very bad manners, because the card represents the person.

And, while we're on the subject of giving and taking, the Japanese do this with both hands. Using one hand only is considered very offhand.

The Japanese will smile at everyone, whether they like them or not. So smiles do not guarantee that you have been accepted.

The trick in Japan is to get acquainted, before sitting down and plunging into the business discussions. There is no way that they will put their cards on the table at the start. Rather, they will first send a scout to reconnoitre the terrain, then they will send in some more troops and, depending on the deal, one may see many more soldiers before the higher ranks of the company arrive.

This is why many US companies have problems doing business with the Japanese. The preliminaries may seem interminable but, once they are satisfied, they decide promptly and en masse.

Doing business with the Japanese is about (1) building up a relationship and (2) status.

During conversations, do not be alarmed by the silence. Unlike our Mediterranean nations who will interrupt at any time, the Japanese will listen until the other person has finished speaking, they will courteously digest in silence what has been said, and then they will respond.

Business will be conducted only in the Friendly Business Aura. It will probably take years to get there – and you'll need to learn Japanese, before you have a chance of entering their Friendly Personal Aura.

The Thais, Singaporeans and Malaysians

Thailand, Singapore and Malaysia are countries where the customers are treated as the most important people in the world – and it's not only for the money. There are so many examples of this special brand of Tender Loving Care, that we've found it difficult to choose what to give you.

> Breakfasting in an hotel in Thailand, Ron was surprised to find himself being gently quizzed as to the precise amount of sugar or sweetener he would like – if any. And then he watched the waiter carefully place one lump of brown sugar in his coffee, and stir it gently until it was dissolved.

If you really want to learn about customer service, fly with Thai or Singapore airlines. They go to such extremes that poor, benighted Europeans may find themselves quite overwhelmed.

> On Ron's first trip to the Far East, in the early 80s, the outward flight was with Singapore Airways, and the return flight with a European carrier, whose name we won't mention.
>
> On the flight out, he was welcomed on board and shown to his seat by a Chinese stewardess who lived in Singapore. He was so excited by the fact that he was going to the Far East that he couldn't sleep a wink. All his fellow-passengers were fast asleep, which was reasonable as this was a night-flight from Amsterdam. In the middle of the night, the same stewardess came up to him and asked whether he needed a sleeping pill. Not wanting to sleep, he asked her if she would, instead, tell him something about Singapore and Thailand. This was a woman with a History Degree, and she spent two hours, not only telling him the trivial things one can find in the guidebooks, but the history of both countries. Finally, and apologising profusely, she said she had to have some sleep herself – as is the custom for the crew on long hauls.
>
> This experience was in stark contrast to the return flight with the European airline. Ron asked a stewardess politely for a glass of water; so in the middle of the night, while most of the passengers were asleep, she shouted down the aisle to a colleague: 'the guy in seat K96 wants a glass of water'. Welcome back to reality!

Doing business in these countries is a different ball game from most European countries or the USA.

Price negotiations when shopping can take ages. It took Ron well over two hours to negotiate the price of a statue down to 30% of the marked price in Singapore. Whatever the item, bargaining has to be done – otherwise business is no fun. There will always be smiles, and there may be cups of tea. By haggling, the buyer is showing respect for the culture; and, by producing tea, the seller is showing respect for the buyer's bargaining skills.

And, of course, this applies to business too. It's a part of their culture – that's how they do things. It's a game, it's fun. Play it, and enjoy it. You'll probably be doing it in Friendly Business. Friendly Personal is preferable, but it takes some doing.

The Indians

Ron has done business with many Indians, but not in India. He finds them to be very honourable people.

India is a deeply spiritual country, and we have already discussed the question of what to wear in order to show respect for this spirituality.

One important thing – if you need to get about, hire a driver, rather than taking your life into your own hands when confronted by bullock carts doing U-turns on the motorway in the middle of the night. Indian drivers are used to each other's habits – they think nothing of overtaking on bends on mountain roads, and everyone drives in the middle of the road so, if you want to overtake, you just have to sound your horn. All this makes driving altogether too nerve-racking and noisy for most foreigners.

The Middle East

Europeans think that their history is vastly superior to the Americans', but Mesopotamia (between the Euphrates and Tigris rivers and now part of Iraq) is thought to be the site of the earliest civilisation. The Jews are in their 5th millennium of living in the Middle East, the Egyptians built their first pyramid in 2665BC and Cyrus established the Persian Empire in 550 BC – all of which makes us look like upstarts.

Any and all effort we can put into learning about the history and culture of any region we are to visit in the Middle East will stand us in good stead.

Remember the disappointment and disgust of the stallholder in Monty Python's Life of Brian when someone paid the full price without haggling?

This is expected of you in business: be prepared, and keep your cool. If you play your cards right, and master the unwritten rules, you may become a most respected business partner.

In this area, it is relationship building that counts, and business is preferably done in the Friendly Personal Aura.

The Israelis

We have given the Israelis a section of their own because Israel is an extraordinary mix of people from all over the world. They aim to excel at whatever they do, in order to survive.

In business, they are tough and, especially when they communicate in English, can come over as rather aggressive.

The first encounters with Israelis can be very cold and it takes several meetings to melt the ice, and, even then, one has to be aware that the melted ice may freeze over again instantly if they feel offended. They have very pronounced defence barriers, which is not surprising when one takes their history into account, but being introduced by a Jew or another Israeli can work wonders.

Although they may look scruffy and behave chaotically, never underestimate their knowledge. They are very creative in business, as well as in technology, and they always make sure that they are up to date. They can be very critical, not only of outsiders, but also of themselves.

For the Israelis, humour is essential in business, but not at the first meeting – because it might come across as lacking in sincerity. Their humour is not very easy to grasp and, if in doubt, just forget about it.

Once a bond is created, it may be for life, and long-term business is conducted only in the Friendly Personal Aura; but to get there may take longer than swimming the Atlantic.

The Iranians

Iran is a very beautiful country, with some of the friendliest people one can meet. Maybe, within ten years, it could become a favourite tourist destination, albeit alcohol-free.

Three recommendations for business travellers:

1. If you need a car, employ a driver: Iranians are terrifying behind the wheel.

2. If you're out and about, keep a supply of loo paper about your person.
3. If you talk finance up front, you can forget about any deals, now and in the future.

The Iranians make excellent business partners. Start by building a relationship based in the Friendly Personal Aura as soon as you arrive and, when this is established, you can start to talk business.

The South Africans

Many years ago, during apartheid, Ron visited an agricultural site. The Managing Director showed him round. The MD was white and all the labourers were black. His behaviour was completely alien to Ron: the way he shouted at his labourers was reminiscent of Second World War movies and, on top of that, he was carrying a gun. He told Ron that, if they didn't obey him, he would start by firing a warning shot into the air.

Now, many years later, these people are trying to rebuild their country and there is no reason for them to believe that all white people are 'nice'. They have their own problems as well – whether or not these are the after-effects of apartheid. As with communism, the past cannot be dismissed overnight, and it may take many generations before they can actually forget the past and live in harmony with one another.

Business can certainly be done in South Africa, although we need to allow time for trust to develop.

The USA

We both know many Americans and they are the most warm-hearted people one could hope to meet. If you like huge hugs, get yourself some American friends.

Hospitality, friendliness, understanding, and openness to new ideas aptly describe these people. And our friends are extremely keen to learn about other cultures.

Having said all this, we need to remember the size and wealth of the United States. The Americans have become rich by doing business the way they do it. Therefore the way that they do business must the 'the one right way'. It stands to reason, doesn't it? Why would they want to think any differently? It is not until they find themselves failing to get business in the rest of the world that they start asking themselves questions about what they could do differently.

If we had a Social CAT, we could say that Friendly Social (equates to Friendly Business) and Friendly Personal are intertwined in the USA; in other words, once you're in Friendly Social, access to Friendly Personal is easily available – not so in business, where the two first auras are opened up, but never Friendly Personal.

This is the big difference between doing business in the USA and in Europe – where social and business approaches overlap. The British industrialist, Sir John Harvey-Jones, who was one of the models for Diana's *NLP for Lazy Learning*, found the Americans quite bewildering: when he gives his friendship, he gives it for life; but he found that, in the USA, people would fête him, wine him and dine him until the contract was signed – and that was the last he'd ever see of them.

The USA is a vast country and, as we saw earlier, only 10% of its inhabitants have passports. It appears, as far as business is concerned, that the sun rises in New York and sets in Los Angeles, and that the rest of the world – if it does exist – is highly suspect.

This was illustrated by a cardiovascular surgeon, whom Ron met in Tehran. He was born in Kashmir, educated in the UK and in the USA (Stanford University), and was now living in Denver, Colorado, where he found it very easy to get acquainted with the locals – so he was having a brilliant time, socially. But work was quite different; and one of the problems was that his colleagues could not understand why on earth he would want to travel to other parts of the world to *learn from other cardiovascular surgeons* – when everything one could possibly need could be found in the USA. He was an interesting and highly intelligent man, from whom Ron learned some fascinating things about surgery around the world.

Another thing to be aware of is that, on the whole, Americans show a greater tendency to contribute success to themselves, as individuals, whereas failure is due to external factors or events (BSE = Blame Somebody/thing Else). This is in contrast to Chinese Americans, or Mainland Chinese, who will attribute success *and* failure primarily to themselves. And there is the overriding factor we discussed earlier that, in general, the Americans consider that time is money, that they are focused on money and on the USA, and that long-term planning extends to three months.

141

The Land of Lawyers

One of Diana's favourite American jokes goes:

> Q. A lawyer and a skunk have both been run over. How can you tell which is which?
>
> A. There are skid marks in front of the skunk.

Did you know that, for each lawyer per head of population in Japan, there are 3 in Europe, and 25 in the USA? This explains a lot about the way they do business in the USA, and about the time it takes to build trust in Japan. It also explains the need for trust in the rest of the world.

> In the USA, in the mid-90s, a woman drove into a fast food outlet, and bought herself a beaker of freshly-brewed coffee to go. She put it between her legs, and drove away. When the coffee spilled, and burned her, she sued the company.

When this story broke, the Europeans fell about laughing at the stupidity of the suit. Who would put a cup of hot coffee between their legs in the first place? And who, having been burned themselves through their own stupidity, could imagine that they could legally lay the blame at someone else's door?

When she won the case, the Europeans couldn't get their heads round it at all. But then it was Mr Bumble, in Oliver Twist, who said: 'if the law supposes that, the law is a ass, a idiot'.

The first thing that struck Diana, when she arrived in California, was all the ''Thou Shalt Nots' nailed over the door', as William Blake would have it. 'No roller blading, no smoking, no drinking, no fighting' – wherever you went, the list of prohibitions seemed endless. Not that they wanted to fight, but – as a protest against the infringement of their personal liberties – she and a German friend moved out of their motel, and into a place where there was no interdict against fighting.

The fear of being sued is ever-present and, at one stage, a gang of American consultants was making a fortune in England going round companies and telling them how they should behave. No smiling, no touching, no fraternising after work: all these could be misconstrued as harassment. Professionalism at all times – friendship does not enter into the work equation. No wonder American business people won't let you into their Friendly Personal Aura!

Let's join a typical staff meeting held in Europe, with some of the participants over from HQ in the USA. The Americans are doing the presentations, and the Europeans (including Ron) are listening, or are at least physically present.

The representative of the legal department opens the show, and explains the one thousand different laws they have to obey in the States.

- Thou shalt not talk to thy competitor at all, let alone discuss prices.
- Thou shalt not reveal any information to a third party.
- Thou shalt not steal any software to use at home.
- Thou shalt abide by the environmental laws, by the safety laws, by the security laws, and by the sexual harassment laws.
- Thou shalt not smoke in the office, even if thou hast thine own closed office.
- Thou shalt not drink alcoholic beverages during office hours or at business meals.
- Thou shalt not insult other people.
- Thou shalt follow all the other 990 other laws including antitrust,

By this time, the Europeans have started wondering who the hell they can trust in such an environment, if people won't behave properly unless they are told to.

Then the HR person is wheeled in to explain, in one breath, how people have to trust one another and, in another, how to deal with people according to their position in the company in relation to yours.

'But what', enquired Diana, as Ron was relating this story, 'does trust mean to these people?'

Ron rummages among his papers and produces a list:

1. **Trust is the willingness to depend on someone**. That sounded reasonable.
2. **Trust is not liking someone.** *'What?'* But Ron has no answer to this; the concept had been too much for him and his mind had wandered off, leaving no recollection of any explanation.
3. **Trust is particularly critical in power relationships.** *'Power relationships?'*

   'In power relationships, there are seven different ways of talking to people: prescriptive, auditing, co-ordinative, monitoring, service, advisory and collateral', says Ron.

And, as Diana's eyes glaze over, he gleefully produces a pencil and draws this graph, explaining that how members of this company talked to people would depend upon their position and their relationships to their superiors or subordinates.

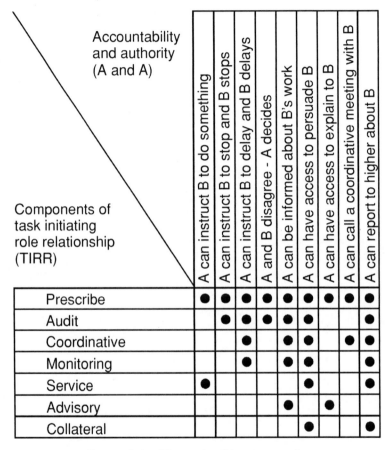

Components of task initiating role relationship (TIRR) \ Accountability and authority (A and A)	A can instruct B to do something	A can instruct B to stop and B stops	A can instruct B to delay and B delays	A and B disagree - A decides	A can be informed about B's work	A can have access to persuade B	A can have access to explain to B	A can call a coordinative meeting with B	A can report to higher about B
Prescribe	●	●	●	●	●	●	●	●	●
Audit		●	●	●	●	●			●
Coordinative			●		●	●		●	●
Monitoring			●		●	●			●
Service	●						●		●
Advisory						●		●	
Collateral							●		●

Figure 8.1 – Ways of talking to people

Diana is trying to bring these complicated instructions down to something she can get her head round.

'*So what happens,*' she enquires during this explanation, '*if I don't like your smoking in my office?*'

'*You complain to my boss.*'

'*But I'd rather tell you up front. I don't like going behind people's backs.*'

Ron looks at her pityingly: '*this system is all about going behind people's backs. So it can be used very effectively to manipulate and fire people.'*

Back to meeting: the Europeans have long since lost all interest because the concept is either laughable or impossible to understand. But they wake up when the finance guy comes on, because they have invested millions of dollars in this project.

The finance guy presents *'la danse des chiffres'*: that well-known ballet of deeply-massaged figures. Using these figures, he demonstrates that they are making a profit on the project, although the Europeans all know that they have made a dramatic loss. And they talk about trust!

It is useful to remember at this stage that it is the American Richard Bandler (who created NLP) who maintains: *'there's only one problem in this world: people take themselves too goddam seriously.'*

The Mid-West

The Mid-West seems to be world of its own. The Mid-West is a confusing name: Left-of-centre-North would describe it more accurately, but it could be loosely described as mid-way to the West. It comprises the states to the west and south of the Great Lakes: Ohio, Indiana, Illinois, Michigan, Iowa, Wisconsin, Minnesota, Kentucky and Missouri ('if I can't see it, I won't believe it'). In case you think we're being xenophobic and making everything up, Hutchinson's Encyclopaedia describes this vast area as 'conservative socially and politically, and isolationist'.

It appears that, as far as the inhabitants of the Mid-West are concerned, the rest of the world – and this includes everyone outside their immediate environs – is beyond the pale. Outsiders are a threat; the 'F' word looms, and these people have the most pronounced defence barriers that one will encounter in business – simply because of the size of the country, the homogeneity of the people and the lack of interaction with other cultures.

Ron met some Mid-West Americans from Des Moines who were living in the UK; the husband's company was working in the field of agriculture, as was Ron. These people had never been abroad before. The two men were discussing a project, which involved the recycling of waste wood into a value-added product. Ron was explaining that this project was being developed by some Israelis, when the question came: 'do they have trees in Israel? I thought it was all desert.' If America is the only country in the world worth tuppence, then one can only suppose that Jaffa must be somewhere in California.

('As sure as God's in Gloucestershire': we both live in this beautiful county, in the Mid-West of England, and the country people here are probably not as different from the people of the Mid-West of the USA as one might like to hope. We're both regarded as rather odd: Ron because he's a foreigner, and Diana because she's lived abroad and speaks foreign languages. After all, if God's in Gloucestershire, why would anybody want to be anywhere else?)

Here is a Mid-West story to demonstrate how to lose business without really trying:

Ron was at a meeting between his American company and an international Dutch company, which was the largest in its field in the world at that time. The American company was represented by the CEO (let's call him James), one of the VPs (Henry), a colleague from the European HQ and Ron. The Dutch were represented by two high ranking members of the company (Henk and Hans).

Henk gave a very impressive presentation on their world-wide operations. And, when it came to James's, turn, he began as follows: 'Well Henk, I think you need to learn how to get more transparency into your operation and you should follow the example of ... (a large company in the USA).'

Before James could continue, Henk turned to Ron and said, in Dutch, that the meeting was over, unless James immediately stopped telling him how to run his company.

After profuse apologies, and some very smooth talking, Ron managed to get across to Henry that James was breaking all the bounds of a decent business relationship.

Henk, Hans and Ron, had lunch together later, and Henk (the second-in-command of this multi-billion dollar company) said that, if it hadn't been for Ron's immediate apology, his company would never have done business with Ron's again – the result of which would have been a loss of several million dollars to Ron's company.

'This attitude of feeling superior is so typical of a lot of people who have never seen the world apart from their own little environment. Nonetheless, it is one of the most damaging attitudes in business: the feeling of being superior.' This is a quote from a European businessman, whose name we won't reveal, and we've been pretty scathing about Americans in general, and Mid-Westerners in particular. But, if we stop, and go into 2nd position

with them, we realise that, if you've always done business this way, and always made yourself pots of money, why change the habits of a lifetime?

We also realise that an attitude of superiority is not necessarily their intention: because they don't do business in Personal Auras, they probably don't do 2nd position either, and thus have no idea of the effect of their behaviour upon others. They also have no idea that, if they come across as superior, that makes us feel inferior. And, when we think about it, what we are griping about is only their behaviour: it has nothing to do with who they are. Bringing in lawyers, for example, after we have shaken hands on a deal, implies that they don't trust us; but this is only an implication. This is simply the way they do business. We infer that they don't trust us but what evidence do we actually have?

Once again, we need to be aware that behaviour is just behaviour; and that the way we interpret this behaviour is up to us. It is our choice whether we decide to be mortally offended, or whether we decide to just shrug it off as 'the way they do things', or whether we respond in a completely different way. Our response is our own responsibility.

We hasten to add that this is certainly not a general trait for all Americans. We have come across many delightful people who know more about so many things in Europe than we do. And, we must never forget that Madison, Wisconsin is the birthplace of *'The Onion'* – the wickedly satirical newspaper that specialises in human folly. Apart from the mass of people who buy it, 5 million people world-wide read it on line. So, even in the Mid-West, there is fun to be found, if you know where to look.

Doing business in the USA is pretty sterile in comparison to Europe or the Far East. Talk money, present your case, don't waste time, come to the point straight away and eventually the lawyers will take over to finalise the contract.

Deal done; that's it; we can go home now.

Success Checklist for the rest of the world

1. Thailand is the world's best Customer Service Model.

2. Never underestimate the Japanese!

3. In Japan, the preliminaries may seem interminable. Enjoy them! They're worth it.

4. In Japan, business is about relationship and status.

5. In Asia, haggling is expected of you: don't disappoint them.

6. In the Middle East, head for Friendly Business - and remember to haggle.

7. Israelis are tough business people, and can come across as aggressive.

8. Israelis have powerful defence barriers: get yourself introduced by a Jew or another Israeli, if possible.

9. In Iran, head for Friendly Personal, before talking business.

10. Allow trust to develop in South Africa.

11. The USA is the Land of Lawyers: forget Friendly Personal.

12. For most Americans, the rest of the world hardly exists.

13. The Mid-West is 'conservative and isolationist'.

14. In the USA, talk money, present your case, come to the point straightaway, and it will all be settled by lawyers.

9

One Man's Gift
is Another Man's Poison

If you look up the word 'Gift' in a German dictionary, this is what you will find: 'Gift: nt (lit, fig) poison.' This is an example of linguistic 'false friends', which you'll find out more about later.

Words can mean anything the listener chooses them to mean. The actor, Bernard Cribbins, did a wonderful monologue called: *'I wonder what she meant when she said 'Yes', like that'*, when he rambles on for about five minutes putting every possible interpretation upon one single word.

Language can be very slippery, but it's the best we can come up with in order to create any sort of precision in our communication – and you notice that we say a 'sort of precision'. Language has supposedly made mankind the masters of the world, but the misunderstandings it can create are mind-boggling. We need to remember the advice given to Alice when she went through the looking-glass.

> *'When I use a word,'* Humpty Dumpty said in rather a scornful tone, *'it means just what I choose it to mean – neither more nor less.'*
> *'The question is,'* said Alice, *'whether you can make words mean so many different things.'*
> *'The question is,'* said Humpty Dumpty, *'which is to be Master – that's all.'*

Before we start thinking about misunderstandings, let's think about what language is, what it's for and where it has come from. For example, we could send you off to the market to buy half a dozen eggs by using sign language; but, unless we are all professional signers, communicating the message that we don't want you to get them from that woman on the third stall down on the left hand side, in the second aisle as you go in by the west gate – because her eggs are always old – would take a fair amount of doing. So we use language instead.

The language that each of us uses comes from thousands and thousands of years of culture: we talk in the way that we think (and we think in the way that we talk). Children model their parents, as a way of discovering how to get on in the world; so they take on their parents' language, their tonality and their physiology – and so it goes on for generation after generation.

Different languages will use different expressions, idioms and metaphors, because they think differently. For example, in England, if someone is looking depressed, we'll say 'chin up!'; the Germans will say 'head up!'; the French will wish you courage, but only when they notice an improvement will they say: 'he's looking better. He's got his head up.' Nor will the Spanish advise you to change your physiology. Maybe, in countries with more sunlight, there is less depression, and they don't need to know about the benefits that looking up brings to depression, which we discussed earlier.

The English 'look forward to something'; the French 'await it with impatience'; ' the Spanish 'delight themselves in advance' – each phrase demonstrating an entirely different way of thinking about the future. (One of Diana's clients could not make plans, and a bit of questioning revealed that she visualised the past in front of her, and the future behind her. So she literally had 'nothing to look forward to'.

The vexed question of gender (which English speakers can find so difficult in foreign languages) also gives us great insights into how a culture thinks. In French, feminine things come – in general – under the headings of beautiful, dangerous, expensive and indispensable; for example: water, beer, car, music, electricity, machine, house, chair, table, plant, flower, food, light, faith, birth, life and death. Whereas masculine things are strong and/or useful; for example: coffee, wine, whisky, knife, hammer, train, book, bread, hotel, train, bus, computer, order, word, stamp, marriage. The Germans are not so romantic about their cars: they're masculine or neuter (if you have an *Auto*, rather than a *Wagen*) – but machines, in general, seem to be feminine in a lot of languages.

The English bewilder foreigners by calling ships 'she', which nobody else seems to do – maybe this is because, as a maritime race, they relied upon their ships so much. And, interestingly, although English and Japanese have no genders for 'things', both cultures think of the sun as masculine and the moon as feminine: as do the French, Italians, Spanish and Greeks – but the Germans think of them the other way round.

Speaking another language also *feels* different: the words come from different parts of our body, and our whole physiology is different. For example, try speaking French or Italian without using your hands. If you know the song 'Yes, I remember it well', from Gigi, you can experiment with this, by pretending to be Maurice Chevalier and then Hermione Gingold, as you sing it – or even speak it – and you will discover that it feels as though you are two different people, when you speak English with a French accent, and then with an English one. Alternatively, try imitating anyone's foreign accent, and discover how different you feel. Or try saying words from other languages, and then the translation into your own, and notice where they come from, and how different they feel to you.

Diana and her husband, Philip, were on their way home from a party in France when he asked her why she waved her hands about all over the place when she was speaking French. It was very strange, he opined. Realising that telling him she couldn't speak French with her hands behind her back would come across as ridiculous, she treated the question as rhetorical, and said nothing.

How you process sound

Here is another experiment for you to try: put on some music, and lie down, relax, close your eyes and just allow your eyes to follow the notes. As you do this, you will discover how you have programmed your brain to receive sound. Some people find that their eyes go up as the music goes up – which seems logical – and others find that they follow the scales sideways. As you do this, you may find that your eyes can predict which way the music will go. You may find that your eyes move incredibly fast – like rapid eye movement in dreams. Go with it, and discover what happens.

Once you've discovered how your brain processes music, then you can try closing your eyes and listening to other languages; you'll notice that your eye movements will have different patterns for the music of each language.

'C'est le ton qui fait la musique', as the French would say, or *'it ain't what you say, it's the way that you say it'* It's also the spaces between the notes that make the music, and the same goes for speech, and the art of when to stay silent, in other cultures. Be aware of the tonality of the language that you are in and you will realise, for example, that the Italians are not in the middle of a murderous argument: they're just having a perfectly normal discussion.

Going back to modelling our elders and betters as children: Diana remembers being horrified by the tone of voice that a small child was using to her mother – until she realised that was exactly how the child's father spoke to her mother: that's what Daddy does, it's obviously the right way to do it.

Use the intonation of the other culture, as well as the physiology: for example, if you want to get something done in Germany, use German intonation: absently wondering aloud whether something would be possible – as one would in England – will get you nowhere.

Above all, use the same intonation as the person you are talking to, where possible. People whose voices are moderated can respond adversely to loudness, and interpret it as brashness; people who talk loudly can interpret a quiet voice as timidity. Play it by ear!

It's also useful to be aware of which intonations grate on our own ears, in order that we don't respond unfavourably at an unconscious level. If we compare, for example, German and Indian intonation, and imagine a native speaker of each (who hasn't quite got the hang of English present tenses) saying: 'you are telling me please the way to the station?' (Indian); and 'you are telling me please the way to the station.' (German). The word order does not form a question, so the German, quite correctly, allows his voice to drop at the end of the sentence; this makes it sound like an order, and our instant, unconscious response might be 'who do you think you are, ordering me about like that?'. Whereas, the Indian, incorrectly, raises his voice at the end of the sentence, to make it sound like a question – and we instantly want to help. And all because of the intonation.

English speakers are fortunate in that English is the language most widely used for business (there are 1,500 million English speakers – including those who have it as a second language); and we always need to remember that, for the person we are talking to, it may well be their second, third or even fourth language. Each party may think they have reached an understanding, only to discover later that they have agreed to different things; alternatively, business may be lost through misinterpretation. There are innumerable 'false friends': words that mean different things in different languages; in fact, it is reasonable to assume that, if one language has borrowed a word from another, the meaning has probably changed. For example, '*demander*' means 'to ask' in French. If someone whose first or second language is French should tell us, in English, that he demands a discount of X%, we're not going to respond favourably, unless we are aware that he's just 'asking' for a discount.

And English speakers, learning the history of the Reformed Church at school, will remember the giggles raised by the concept of 'The Diet of Worms'.

Idioms

Idioms don't translate literally, and can cause great confusion for non-native speakers, for example, a henpecked husband is 'a slipper hero' in German but, disappointingly, just 'dominated by his wife' in French and Spanish. And the endless euphemisms for relieving oneself (from 'having to see a man about a dog' in England to 'watering one's horse' in the USA) can flummox a non-native speaker.

The German expression '*Fingerspitzengefühl*', which we discussed earlier, translates as 'Fingertip feeling', meaning an 'instinctive feel'; the Dutch '*Boerenverstand*', which translates as 'Farmers' intelligence', meaning 'common sense'; and the American expressions '*Ballpark figure*' or '*We need to touch base*' or '*The whole nine yards*', are all idiomatic: they cannot be translated literally, and will only serve to confuse non-native speakers.

The trick, when talking business abroad, is to eliminate what is idiomatic, and to speak good clear English: the language that they have been taught.

Cultural business conversation differences

Ron compares conversing with the **Italians, Spanish** and other **Latin** races to a trip to the opera: all the drama is there, as well as the music.

German conversation is straight, and no-nonsense: business is a serious matter.

Dutch is a somewhat limited language, according to Bernard Haitink, the world-famous one-time conductor of the Amsterdam orchestra. Usually when Dutch people speak English they come over as too direct: they call a spade a spade. This can upset their interlocutors, so we need to remember that this is just the way that the Dutch speak and accept it as a fact of life.

The **Chinese** and **Japanese** use beautiful metaphor – mostly related to nature. As we saw earlier, they would never dream of suggesting directly that one 'be more flexible', they would try to get their message across by mentioning 'bending like a willow rather than breaking like a rose tree.'

We need to be very impressed when we come across Chinese and Japanese English speakers: learning English, or any other European language come to that, is a different concept for them.

In Chinese, for example, each character represents a word rather than a letter. There are no tenses: they speak in the present with past/future marker, for example: 'yesterday, I go town', or 'tomorrow, I go town'. To speak English, they have to get used to the monstrous business of verbs' changing according to time. Also, Chinese is a tonal language: there are five tones, which can give one syllable five different meaning.

So, if the Chinese have shown us the respect of learning English, they deserve lots of respect in return.

In Japanese, there is the formal language and the friendly one. As one might expect, the former is used in business and the latter amongst friends. Japanese women also have their own language, which they speak among themselves.

The **English** like to keep things vague, and – as Ron likes to say – use more nuances than there are colours in a Monet painting. Because the English don't like discussing business until the third act, Ron is convinced that only they could have so many idioms around the concept of coming, or not coming, to the point: *'beating about the bush'*, *'making a meal of it'*, *'going round in circles'*, *'taking the bull by the horns'*, *'calling a spade a spade'*, *'to cut a long story short'*, *'to put it in a nutshell'*, and so on.

The **Americans** like things simple and straight: what you hear is what you get – and they do have a passion for long words: why say simply 'transport', when you can call it 'transportation'?

Norn Irn is how 'Northern Ireland' is pronounced at home, and as John Pepper of The Belfast Telegraph had it: 'English almost spoken here'. *'Us day dawn!'* confused Diana when she first went to live there, but she rapidly realised that it was 'that's dead on!' or 'absolutely right'. The Irish, being the friendly nation that they are, will (as soon as they realise they can trust you) immediately take you to their bosom and use their normal language: be prepared to enjoy the confusion; and, when a shop assistant in the North says 'Nigh' to you, you'll know it's your turn 'now' to be served. Norn Irn has a wonderful collection of otherwise lost Elizabethan words in its vocabulary (although some of them still exist in the States).

In an earlier chapter, we looked at 'register': the language one uses according to the formality or informality of the conversation. Once again, this is a question of listening and allowing the other person to set the level of the conversation: if they want to keep it formal, that's fine; and, if they want to use less formal language, that's fine too.

And, of course, there are different levels of vocabulary according to class, so we need to be careful about using language we've picked up from street vendors, when we're talking to the nobility. Fortunately, foreigners are generally very kind about such lapses, and will enquire interestedly about where we learned such a word, and explain to us that it's not suitable for polite conversation, or that it's slang, or whatever.

British English/US English

There is enough room for misunderstanding between English speaking nations to fill a book. British English is taught in most European countries, and the English are liable to complain loudly about the invasion of modern Americanisms into their language – not realising that American English has the older pedigree, and dates from Shakespearean times (see the bibliography for Bill Bryson's *Mother Tongue*). This, of course, excludes the truly modern American language of computers, and so on.

In the mid 80s, an engineer showed Ron a technical English/American dictionary, and he was astounded by the size of this *œuvre*. Here are a few everyday examples of possible confusion between the two languages.

British English	American English	Translation into British English
W.C.; Toilet	Restroom	Room for resting
Give way (traffic sign)	Yield	Give up, surrender
Caravan	Trailer	Vehicle for towing
Bonnet of car	Hood	Head cover
Boot of car	Trunk	Large case for packing clothes
Indicator	Blinker	Someone who blinks
Car silencer	Muffler	Woolly scarf
Tights	Pantyhose	
Pavement	Sidewalk	
Motorway	Freeway	
Beer mat	Coaster	Wine bottle holder that glides round the table

False Friends

As we saw above, there are lots of words that we think we know, but which mean something completely different in another language. Middle English was much more like German, and it wasn't until after the arrival of the Normans, when French was spoken at Court, that we got to Modern English. So between French and English there can be great confusion; although, interestingly, 'false friends' translates directly into French as *'faux amis'*.

English word	Meaning in French	French word	Meaning in English
Sensible	Raisonnable	Sensible	Sensitive to
To assist	Aider	Assister	be present
Exhibition	Exposition	Exhibition	Flaunting display
Shopping trolley	Chariot	Char	Chariot/tank
Isolation	Isolement	Isolation	Insulation
To check	Controller	Maitriser	To control

If a Frenchmen said: *'our new isolation material is exposed at the salon'*, he would mean: *'our new insulation material is being exhibited at the trade fair'*. So you won't laugh, will you, when you hear about the sculptresses exposing their busts in the salon.

Ship or Sheep?

The difficulties that foreigners find in distinguishing between the 'i' and 'ee' sounds in English can lead to even more confusion. Diana, helping to organise a charity picnic in the Loire Valley, was asked to put the sheeps out. Surprised, she looked around for sheep to evict, but there weren't any; and, as they were miles from the sea, ships were unlikely. Eventually she realised that potato crisps ('chips' – another false friend) were the subject under discussion. And, years ago, when she was running a summer school for foreign children learning English, she found, carved deep into a desk, the classic example of this lack of distinction: 'Ahmed is a big sheet'.

Forms of address

We have already discussed this, at some length in Chapter 2, so this is just a reminder that we need to wait to be invited to call people by their first names; and also to address them by the formal version of 'you', until asked to do otherwise. As in France, some Dutch parents may insist that their children address them with the formal 'U'; whereas, in Spain, you, as a stranger, may quickly find yourself on 'tu' terms. As we said earlier, it's all about respect; and, without showing respect, one can easily lose the deal.

Guten Appetit!

In most cultures, people wish one another a good appetite before starting a meal, for example: *Bon appétit* in France, *Smakelijk* in the Netherlands, *Smacznego* in Polish, and so on; whereas in Anglo-Saxon cultures virtually nobody utters a word. *'Dig in'* may not have the same connotation. This little ceremony has so much importance that, at a formal dinner in France, Ron saw the host waiting for ages, because nobody had said the magic words.

Very slowly, the habit of saying, 'Enjoy your meal' is creeping into some pubs and restaurants, no doubt encouraged by the more positive continental practice.

A little effort goes a long way

On one of Ron's first visits to Finland, when he was working for a medical company, he called at a hospital and presented his product to a cardiac specialist.

In general, the Finns speak Suomi (Finnish) and Swedish. There is no reason to speak English when one lives next to the Arctic Circle. Ron presented his product in English, and the good Doctor said kindly – as he showed him to the door – that, if he wanted to be successful, he'd better do something about his limited language skills.

On his next visit, Ron was armed with his Berlitz Suomi-English dictionary. Suomi is not an easy language but, fortunately, as a lot of the discussion was technical, it was mostly just a question of changing the endings: 'serum' became 'serumi', and so on. Ron presented his product in toddler-like Suomi, and the Doctor enjoyed the entertainment so much that he became an excellent customer. The brochures were translated into Finnish, and Ron wonders to this day whether the Doctor had understood anything of what he was trying to tell him.

The purpose of this story is to illustrate that a basic knowledge of the other parties' languages can only enhance our success in business; it also means that one can understand the gist of a discussion, which is a great help. If we operate world-wide, speaking the language of all our business partners is too tall an order, but the more understanding of other languages we can gain can only serve us in good stead.

It all comes back to respect. If we have made the effort, not only are we showing respect, we are also gaining it.

Acronyms and business jargon

One of the major problems when talking business is that too many people use business jargon and acronyms. This is fine at home (provided people understand, which is frequently, and sadly, not the case) but, once we take them abroad, we can find ourselves in trouble as things can translate disastrously. The classic example of different meanings in another culture is the Nova car: nice name, it means 'new' in Latin, so it combines the concept of fresh, new ideas with the pedigree and beauty of ancient Rome. The manufacturers couldn't understand why the Mexicans wouldn't buy their wonderful new car, until they discovered that, unfortunately, 'no va' also means that it doesn't go.

Ron discovered this phenomenon early in life, when his maths teacher used a geometrical example: the vector 'pd op cd' (Dutch for: PD on CD). He was in a mixed class of Dutch and French children. The French laughed their heads off at the teacher's announcement, as what they heard was: 'Pédé obsédé', which means 'obsessed homosexual'.

Jargon and acronyms just provide more traps for the unwary – ban them, as a matter of principle, from all business conversations when abroad.

As always – and we cannot stress this too much – we need to check that we and the other person have understood one another, at every stage of the discussion. If they didn't understand a word the first time round, use a different word, or draw them a picture: do something different to get your message across, because finding anomalies at a later date can only lead to bad feeling.

Lazy Language Learning

It is a truth, universally acknowledged, that most English speakers believe they are missing that part of the brain stamped 'foreign languages' that people like the Dutch and the Belgians were born with – so it's not their fault that they can't learn languages. The Dutch and Belgians speak 'the basic five' as a matter of course: English, French, German, Dutch and Flemish – and think nothing of it. So here are some thoughts for benighted English speakers, who believe that they are incapable of speaking another language.

Have you ever found yourself being surprised at how well French children speak French, or German children speak German? Language learning is easy, provided we relax and enjoy it. This is how children do it.

- They want to communicate.
- They concentrate on the communication, rather than the language.
- They copy other people.
- They use trial and error until they are understood.
- Everything they say is praised and encouraged.
- They are learning in a safe environment.
- People let them talk without correcting them all the time.
- They were born with an understanding of how language works.
- They don't have to learn how to conjugate regular verbs before they're allowed to speak.
- They are allowed to learn in their own way.

So, remembering the above, all you need is to be prepared to do things a bit differently. And, while we're on the subject of children, remember how Ron wanted his children to be able to watch Dutch television, because they spoke no English? If you listen to them now, you would have no inkling that they were not English born and bred: there is not a trace of accent. Nor is there a trace of accent in their Dutch. Children are so wonderfully flexible that they can achieve anything they set their minds to. And, as the Duchess in *Alice's Adventures in Wonderland* would have it: *'Take care of the sense, and the sounds will take care of themselves.'*

Let's go back to Logical Levels again and apply them to the need, or the wish, to speak another language, as a reminder of what you can do to make language learning simple, fun and rewarding.

Environment: Where?	In another country; with people who don't speak our language
When?	When we want to get a message across to someone who doesn't speak our language
Behaviour: what?	In order to speak another language, we need to think and behave differently
Capability: how?	We take on the behaviour, physiology, intonation, etc, of the other person: we nod when they nod, we smile when they smile, and so on. And, when we do this, we astonish

	ourselves by how much more we understand.
Beliefs: why?	This person matters to us; this place matters to us; we want to understand it all at a deeper level; and we want to be able to communicate with them
Identity: who?	We find ourselves taking on a different identity in a different language. By doing this, we enrich who we are.
Who else?	We show others respect, and receive it in return. We expand our circle of close friends, and thereby enrich our lives

Some thoughts on identity

Diana has a theory that one of the reasons that the English are so hopeless at learning foreign languages is that they are afraid they will lose their identities. The opposite is true: as we saw above, if we enrich our identities, we enrich our lives.

The main trick with language learning is to distract the conscious mind – which is always to ready to point out our mistakes, or the possibility that we might make a mistake, should we open our mouths. We can do this by concentrating on the other person, and on getting our message across (which is, after all, far more important than grammar).

An effective way of doing this is to take part in an activity (in the foreign language) which will occupy our conscious minds. For example, Diana learned most of her French either on a horse or round the bridge table. Concentrating on something else keeps the conscious mind occupied with other things, and it forgets to interfere.

Another useful trick is to listen, watch and feel for the sense of the whole idea – as we do in our own language – rather than listening word for word. If we do the latter, and there is a word we don't recognise, we can lose the rest of the sentence because we're panicking about one word. Think of all those people who don't listen to your ideas, but pounce upon one word and start tearing it to bits – and you'll know what we mean. As we said earlier, words only make up about 7% of our actual communication; there is so much else to give us clues; and, anyway, we all repeat ourselves endlessly so, if you missed a word the first time round, its meaning will soon become clear. Remember the perceptual positions exercise, and how much information you gleaned by pretending to be someone else? If we go into second position with the person we are talking to, we pick up masses of information, and discover the meaning at a different level.

Above all, have fun! A foreign language is a whole new world, explore and enjoy it.

Success Checklist

1. Use simple language.

2. Make sure you have understood each other at every stage.

3. If you have been misunderstood, explain things in a different way.

4. Avoid all idioms, and expressions you're not certain about.

5. Avoid all acronyms or business jargon.

6. Listen for the meaning of the whole sentence, rather than individual words.

7. Learn some words and/or sentences of their language just to demonstrate that you have tried.

8. Mistakes are just mistakes. It's your effort that they will appreciate; and this appreciation is worth a lot more than money can buy.

9. Remember you may be expressing yourself in a language foreign to your hosts or guests - speak slowly and clearly.

10. Remember that some words translated into the language of your host or guest may have a totally different meaning.

11. And most important *'C'est le ton qui fait la musique'*, people can respond unfavourably to the 'wrong' intonation.

10

How to Use the Toolbox

Up to now, we've been preparing for our first meeting; so what have we done so far, and what have we got?

- We've done our research on the country and its culture; the company and its culture, and the different ways of doing business in the country.
- We know how to create a hybrid paradigm to suit all parties.
- Applying the Cultural Auras Theory, we know what aura to head for, in order to establish the relationship we need.
- We have an idea about how long it might take to establish this relationship.
- We know where we might find barriers, and how to overcome them.
- We are sensitive to what might be stopping them from wanting to do business with us.
- We know about the pitfalls of language.

So, armed with all this, let's go to our first meeting, move on to negotiating, and then conclude our business. And, as we do this, we need to remind ourselves that each of these is a process – rather than a thing. Each has a beginning, a middle and an end; and we form a part of the system that is the process. In other words, everything that we do is going to affect that process.

The first business encounter

The first encounter is all-important because, if it fails, we might just as well go home and do something else. Not all first meetings are successful, of course; and sometimes they can go wrong as a result of external factors; for example, if you've time to spare, go by air.

Back in the 80s, when he was based in Brussels, Ron made an appointment to see the technical director of a large multinational in the United Kingdom (whom we'll call William). Ron was to be joined by a colleague, the Vice-

President of Research and Development based in St. Louis, USA (whom we'll call Robert). Robert particularly wanted to be there, because William was one of the most important people in their field at the time. When Ron arrived at London Heathrow airport from Brussels, he found that Robert's flight had been delayed by an hour or so.

Knowing that they were behind schedule, they rang William's secretary from the airport. And, of course, the traffic into central London moved at its usual crawl. When they eventually arrived, they were indeed late, and William said bluntly: 'You are 15 minutes late. The meeting is over.' And that was that.

This may sound somewhat extreme, but it's true. William was a stickler for punctuality; so, for him, being late was the ultimate demonstration of rudeness. While you might not go to such extremes, it is useful to remember that there are people who do. In fact, if we bear in mind that we're all different, and we're all barking mad (in one way or another), we'll be well prepared to expect the unexpected.

As a postscript to this story, Ron and William are still on excellent terms, as William subsequently became a very good customer.

First impressions are crucial, as people may decide within a split second whether this is someone with whom they may wish to do business – or not. So let's stop and remind ourselves what happens in the first split second of our meeting with a stranger.

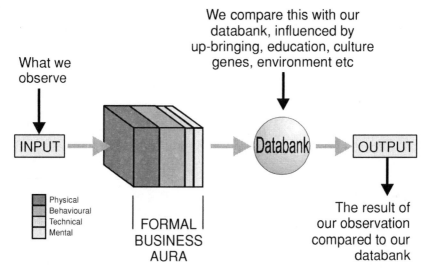

Fig 10.1 – How our minds process first impressions

Figure 10.1 shows how we register the first input we get into our five senses from the person we meet: what we see, hear, feel, taste and smell. We compare and contrast this input with the information in our personal databanks, and the output is our response.

In mathematical terms we could write this as an equation ...

$$\text{Output (total)} = \frac{\textbf{Input (external factors)}}{\textbf{Databank (external factors)}} + \frac{\textbf{Input (internal factors)}}{\textbf{Databank (internal factors)}}$$

... where the External factors are Physical and Behavioural and the Internal Factors are Technical and Mental (see sub-auras).

The all-important first impression is generally formed by external factors (unless, of course, we're feeling terrible ourselves, and our internal state precludes absorbing anything from anybody).

Presupposing that we are feeling good, and that all our senses are open to what is there, one of the following may happen:

(1) Input > databank ... or
(2) Input < databank.

In the case of (1), the input is greater than our databank, and what we observe does not fit in with what we expected. We will attach a very high importance to our first impressions, i.e. the physical and behavioural characteristics of the other person; for example, the lack of smile, the timid voice, the limp handshake, and the smell of garlic may be outside the scope of what we are expecting. Faced with the unexpected, our mouths may dry up and put us off our stroke.

In the case of (2), the input is smaller than our databank and is therefore simply accepted: it just is, and we attach little importance to it. People with broad experience and open minds are generally in 'I know nothing' mode; in other words, their databanks are always open to new information which they absorb like sponges, and the question of judgement doesn't arise.

The trick is to take responsibility for these first impressions ourselves, and to open our minds with pleasure and excitement to whatever we come across, because it is our response to the situation that is going to affect the rest of the meeting.

Let's take an example of input overwhelming the databank.

Many years ago Ron invited a colleague and his wife to the UK. He had travelled a fair amount, but she had never set foot outside Missouri, USA.

Monique (Ron's wife), who likes to dress according to the fashion in Paris, London or Rome – depending on where she has been most recently – was wearing a fairly short skirt for their first meeting: it was nothing dramatic, just slightly above the knee, but it was outside the scope of the female visitor's databank for how respectable wives dressed; so much so that she asked her husband later whether Monique was really Ron's wife, or someone from an escort agency!

In international business we cannot afford to be overwhelmed by these situations, so we need to learn to accept a wide variety of inputs – otherwise we might as well shoot ourselves in the foot right away. So, let's apply CAT and everything we have discussed in previous chapters to our first business meeting.

We're going to imagine that our first encounter is with an alien from another planet – who somehow speaks our language.

Our first task is to understand where this alien is coming from – both physically and mentally. We shall then import these data into our own environment and produce a hybrid paradigm, satisfactory to both parties, which we can then export and set into motion.

Information gathered before our meeting:

- an understanding of their environment
- an understanding of the cultural factors that will have an impact on our doing business
- an understanding of the way they think
- an understanding of the language(s) they will use to communicate with us
- more importantly, the way they use this language.

But, first, let's stop and think about what puts *us* off doing business with someone. Here's a selection of reasons why you might not want to pursue a proposition that someone has made to you – they all relate to the other person's behaviour:

- too superficial, i.e. not interested in me as a person
  - seemed unable to take his/her eyes off my cleavage/tie
  - made ill-educated, disrespectful and stupid remarks about my culture
- too pushy – tried to hustle me into doing business
- made me feel inferior

- too obsequious
- talked 'at' me, rather than to me
- pompous: used too many long words
- droned on and on about technicalities
- talked money up front
- jumped to conclusions without thinking
- tried to tell me how to run my business.

There will be plenty of things you could add to this list.

What can go wrong in a Presentation?

Our first meeting can be equated to a presentation – even if we may not get around to presenting our product until a later date, we are presenting ourselves. Some people are terrified of making presentations, some people love it; and the difference lies in how they think about it.

So let's start about thinking about the system that is a presentation: we have the presenter, and we have the audience of one or more people. So how are we going to think about our audience? For a start, here are some questions?

- Are they here to ridicule us?
- Are they here to make us feel inferior?
- Are they here because they were ordered to be here?
- Are they here because they've got nothing better to do?
- Are they here to make our lives a misery?

And any other questions you can think of, or

- Are they here because they're interested?
- Do they like meeting new people?
- Are they here because we have something useful to offer them?
- Are they prepared to enjoy our presention?

Which way do you want to think about your audience? The choice is up to you.

Focus for the first meeting

So how are we going to behave at our first meeting with our alien? And what are we going to focus on?

- Take our big safe space (which we learned how to create in Chapter 6) into the meeting with us. This enables us to invite the alien into our space, so that he or she will feel welcome, appreciated and safe.

- Remember throughout: *'this person really matters to me'*. In other words, we are creating rapport at identity level. The green skin, the one eye, the four arms and the curious aluminium foil clothing are irrelevant: it's the person we want to get to know.

- As it's the person we want to get to know, we can show respect for any or all of his/her ideas (and, anyway, this alien may be far senior to us, so it's worth it).

- Remember: this is a new culture, we are here to enjoy and to learn.

- Demonstrate how much we are enjoying the new culture; if appropriate tell the alien that we know little about it (this will explain away any cultural gaffes we might commit – and people are very forgiving if they know that we don't know any better).

- Copy the alien's behaviour – this not only creates rapport, but also keeps our own behaviour within cultural bounds.

- Small talk may be very important at this stage: go with the flow.

- Show interest in the alien's background, family, hobbies etc.

- Gauge, from our knowledge of time, trust, etc, in different cultures, the right moment to present our business (this might be several meetings later).

- When the time is right, introduce our company and its activities in a way that will interest the alien, according to the information we have already gathered.

- Explain our product/service clearly and simply, and pay particular attention to the responses. If the alien wants to get technical, that's fine; if not, keep it simple.

- Listen to whatever the alien may have to say, at any time, and put everything into context.

- If our alien has not understood something, explain it again in a different way; for example, if the alien is visual, draw a picture, instead of using words.

- Keep focusing on the alien's technical abilities.

- Analyse what the alien has said, to make sure we have understood correctly, and repeat anything that needs repeating.

● Ensure that the alien has understood us correctly.

● By now, not only will we have explained our product or service fully, we'll also have a feeling of the alien's approach to business; so we can ask him or her for thoughts on the way forward – as a respected future colleague.

We talk a lot about 'respect', and this means is that we really care about the other party; we want them to feel comfortable and at ease throughout. Our dream, beyond the dream for today, is a sound, long-term relationship, leading to ongoing business way into the future.

One more thing to remember, while we're thinking about aliens: **we can't change other people; what we can change is our responses to them.**

To summarise: at our first meeting, we need to focus on:

1. building rapport by making it easy for the alien to be at ease
2. analysing whether it is essential to continue building up a sound relationship rather than talking business
3. explaining our business as simply as possible
4. listening at all times to the alien's input and analysing the responses
5. summarising each step, to ensure understanding on both sides
6. summarising and understanding the next steps; for example, whether there is a need to build the relationship further, or to talk more business, or any other activity which will make the alien interested in whatever we have to offer.

We have used an alien in this example, because we have all found ourselves entrapped by:

1. the unusual appearance or behaviour of the person we were meeting
2. their use of language which bore little relation to what we are used to
3. their inner defence systems, conscious or unconscious, which have separated us
4. not achieving our goals which were the sole purpose of the meeting
5. not listening, and not understanding what has been said
6. jumping to conclusions and assuming others think and act like we do.

The purpose of the first meeting

As with all projects, we need to know what our outcome is. For example, there's no point in going shopping, unless we know what we need to buy;

otherwise, we'll come home with a trolley-load of stuff we don't want, and without what we need.

Our outcome for the first meeting is quite simple: we want to pave the way for the move from the Formal Business Aura into the Friendly Business Aura, where we can actually do business (or, in some countries, the Friendly Personal Aura). This will take as long as it takes, according to the culture. So, in most cultures, all we want to achieve by the end of the first meeting is our new colleague's agreement to another meeting.

As always, we are demonstrating respect, and this can be done effectively by concentrating on, and appreciating, the technical sub-aura.

We're on their territory, so we play their game; and, if several more meetings are required before we are accepted into Friendly Business, then that's the way we'll do it – and enjoy it.

Negotiating

You will notice that we talk about 'negotiating', rather than 'negotiation'. This is because, as we saw above, negotiating is a process, rather than a thing. The system we have created in Formal Business is developing and growing into a different system (Friendly Business or Friendly Personal) from which we can do excellent business. And, as we saw earlier, it is advisable to get as close to the Friendly Personal Aura as possible when negotiating.

As we move into Friendly Business, we discover that the Physical and Behavioural Sub-Auras have lost their importance; it is now the Technical and Mental Sub-Auras that take precedence.

The purpose of negotiating

Our outcome is to achieve an agreement with which all parties involved are satisfied. But we need to remember that the other side may have a hidden agenda. For them, the success of this particular negotiation may not only have a financial importance, in many cultures it may also elevate the negotiator to a higher social status – regardless of the financial aspects.

Therefore, as with every other stage of our campaign, we need to do our homework, and the first question we need to ask ourselves is: *'What is the other person's objective?'*

1. Is it to obtain an elevation in social status?
2. Is it to address someone's ego?

3. Is it political?
4. Is it simply financial?
5. Is it a combination of any or all of the above?

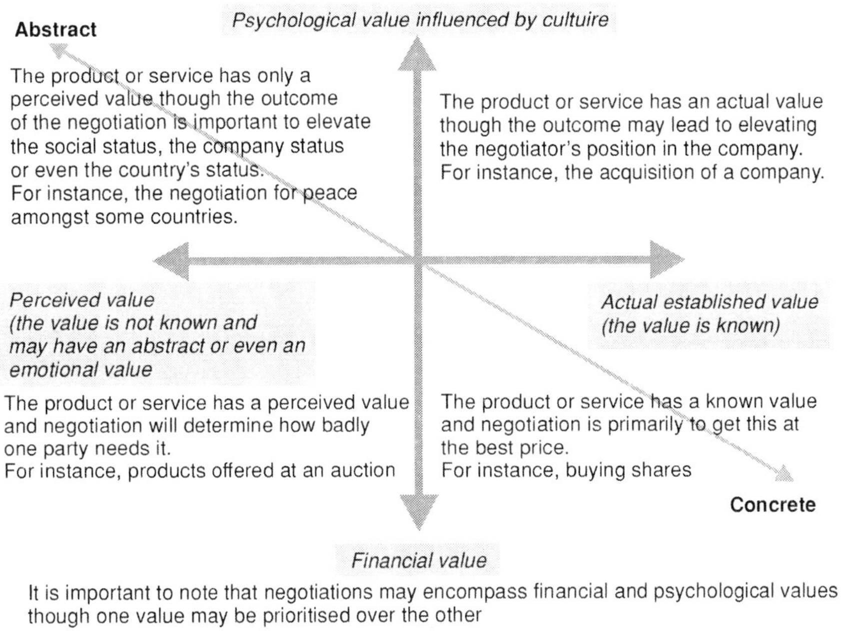

Abstract

Psychological value influenced by cultuire

The product or service has only a perceived value though the outcome of the negotiation is important to elevate the social status, the company status or even the country's status. For instance, the negotiation for peace amongst some countries.

The product or service has an actual value though the outcome may lead to elevating the negotiator's position in the company. For instance, the acquisition of a company.

Perceived value (the value is not known and may have an abstract or even an emotional value

Actual established value (the value is known)

The product or service has a perceived value and negotiation will determine how badly one party needs it. For instance, products offered at an auction

The product or service has a known value and negotiation is primarily to get this at the best price. For instance, buying shares

Concrete

Financial value

It is important to note that negotiations may encompass financial and psychological values though one value may be prioritised over the other

Fig 10.2 – Parameters to consider before negotiating

In Figure 10.2 we can see the many reasons for negotiating. These vary from abstract values like elevating one's ego at one extreme, to concrete values like buying an ounce of gold which will appreciate in value, at the other.

The following example illustrates a typical combination of values:

A German sales manager (a charming, sensitive and amusing man) told Ron, back in the 1980s, how in World War II when he was 10 years old, he was living in an orphanage. The Hitler Jugend visited this orphanage and invited all the children to join them, in return for food and a bed. The message was quite clear: if they didn't join, the consequences would be upon their own heads.

He joined. And, as he explained to Ron all those years later, he had no choice. Those of us who have seen the Leni Riefenstahl films about the Hitler Youth will know what a powerful message they put out. If you joined them, you 'belonged': you were someone. For a cold and probably hungry orphan, living in an institution, it must have been irresistible at both the concrete (food and a roof over his head) and abstract '(belonging' to such a powerful organisation) levels.

Negotiating is a question of values which, as we have seen earlier, have a high priority in our thinking. As we can see from Figure 9.2, these can be divided as follows:

- **Abstract values**: for example, to be accepted by our peers, family, society, superiors, self-esteem, etc.
- **Concrete values**: for example, survival, financial rewards, materialistic rewards, etc.
- **A combination of abstract and concrete**: this is what one would expect, although normally one has a higher priority than the other.

We can also see that, within the abstract and concrete values, there are four further divisions that we need to consider.

1. **Actual value:** here we know the value of the product or service: for example, when we acquire a company, we have an understanding of its value (assets, turn-over, profit, etc.)

2. **Perceived value:** here we have little or no understanding of the true value: for example, when we buy a piece of art at an auction, the price is determined by the bidders, and may bear little relation to its value.

3. **Psychological value:** here the prime reason for the purchase is to satisfy our egos: for example, to elevate our social status, or to satisfy our personal feelings. We might buy a piece of art either to satisfy us psychologically, or as a financial investment. In Japan, for instance, the outcome of the negotiation is primarily a psychological one, the social and company status is far more important than the financial one. Whereas in the USA the financial outcome is far more important.

4. **Financial value:** for example, buying shares, solely to invest.

Once we have an awareness of the values at stake in this particular instance, the next thing we need to think about is the cultural influences.

Physical factors	Environmental factors	Intellectual factors	Psychological factors
Health	Financial	Education	Self-respect/
Fitness	Social	Upbringing	esteem
Physique	Political	Ancestors	Ambition
Visual	Religion	Hobbies	Open-
	Experience of		mindedness
	other cultures		Business values
			Male/female
			values
			Speed at which
			decisions are
			made
			Relationship
			Trust

Table 10.1 – Influencing factors

In this table, we have underlined the factors which are influenced by culture. As discussed earlier, the first two columns are the most important in the Friendly Business Aura; and, once we have got into Friendly Personal Aura, the Intellectual and Psychological factors take over.

In order to analyse how the other party understands business as such, here is a useful exercise.

Does he or she understand and trust:

- our company
- our product/service
- the financial aspects
- the terms of our proposal
- our customer service
- the benefit/s of working with us
- the impact on their future of working with us
- the co-operation we are offering
- the impact of a positive or negative outcome
- us.

If the answer to any of the above is 'No', we need to make sure that we re-address these points in a way that will establish further mutual trust.

Trust is not a tangible element and the first question to ask ourselves is: *'do we trust them?'* Because, if we don't, sure as eggs is eggs they won't trust us. What is more, trust is an on-going phenomenon and, once the deal has been struck, we need to ensure that we enhance it if we're looking for long-term business.

How do we ensure that there is understanding (Intellectual factors) and trust (Psychological Factors)? We started off with zero trust at the beginning – simply because we didn't know each other; but, now that we're in Friendly Business, let's stop and think about the people we don't trust, and – more importantly – why. Here are some suggestions, you can add your own to the list. What we're doing here, as we did earlier, is going into second position with a colleague, to discover what is off-putting when negotiating. Here are some suggestions:

- people who oversell
- people who hustle
- people who fudge, and don't answer questions properly
- people who don't take the trouble to understand our point of view and just go on selling
- people who aren't prepared to meet us half way
- people who tell us we've got to sign soon, or we'll lose the deal
- inflexible people
- people who don't look us in the eye (this is a debatable one: for example, in some cultures it may show respect – check out this culture; or the person might process his thinking through sounds, and will therefore turn his best ear towards us out of politeness; he may also need to look from side to side in order to think)
- over-nervous people – what have they got to hide?
- people who won't respond sensibly to criticism.

Having made our list, the next question we need to ask is: do we do any of these things ourselves – thereby putting off prospective buyers?

So, now that we are aware of the pitfalls, how are we going to do the negotiating?

- If possible, we're going to sit beside our colleague, and lay out the proposal in front of us (literally or metaphorically). This means that we are both 'on the same side', and what we are dealing with is a third entity; in other words, if we disagree, it's not each other we are disagreeing with, but the proposal.

- Set out the facts clearly, including strengths and weaknesses.

- Establish a common denominator: in other words, what can we do for them that's going to make them want to do business with us?

- We've already analysed how our colleague is used to negotiating prices and contracts, and we continue with our analysis while negotiating, in case there is something we've missed.

- Discover whether our colleague needs to discuss any issues with other members of the company before continuing.

- Once all this is settled, we can start negotiating.

- Keep exploring and analysing the reactions of our colleague throughout.

- Keep to the facts, but stay flexible.

- Accept any criticisms (in many cultures this is part of the negotiation process) and respond positively to them.

- If more time is needed, accept the fact. That's the way it is!

Using the above, we should be able to conclude the negotiation with success. But we always need to remember the time factor in different cultures. If we are in the Middle East it may have taken us weeks, months, or years to get a first meeting, so we can easily afford some more time to conclude our negotiation.

There is no failure – only feedback

This is another of NLP's powerful presuppositions. If our negotiating didn't work this time, this is simply because there is something else that we need to learn. We can think about what we could have done differently. We could go back to the First Encounter Scenario with the alien, and ask ourselves if there was anything that we missed; we can continue to build the relationship we have created; or maybe we can console ourselves with the fact that the time wasn't right for them – yet.

Be persistent! Hang in there! The relationship is all; and, if the relationship you have built is strong enough, your new colleagues will tell you why they can't do business with you this time. Be patient! You'll get the rewards you deserve, when the time is right.

Success Checklist

1. Take your big, safe space with you.

2. Take responsibility for your own first impressions.

3. Remember throughout: 'this person really matters to me'.

4. Your outcome for the first meeting = agreement to a second meeting (except in the US where a second meeting may not be necessary).

5. Keep it simple and ensure understanding on both sides.

6. Be 'on their side' when negotiating.

7. Be aware of the other's values when negotiating.

8. Stay flexible.

9. If necessary, pretend you have all the time in the world.

10. There's no Failure - only Feedback.

11

Look to Your Laurels!

David, a friend of Diana's, has recently bought a franchise. He's young, hungry and looking for business. He's also extremely personable, and the one thing that comes across strongly is that he loves other people. This, combined with his determination to provide exactly what you need – and even more if possible, means that new customers are coming in at a nice, steady rate. However, some of these new customers tell him that they've been getting abusive telephone calls from their previous supplier (let's call her Sharon), asking how they dare go to someone else. Obviously no one has told her that laurels are not for resting on until one decides to retire.

Laurels are only awarded for a good job done. You have come a long way – figuratively and sometimes literally – to strike your deal; so now is the time to hang a metaphorical laurel wreath on the wall (or, even better, find a bay tree and make a real one: it needs to be the right size to fit your head like a crown) to remind yourself that business is an on-going thing, and that the relationships you have formed need to be nurtured even more assiduously, now that you have got the business – because a mature plant is much more attractive and useful than a seedling. You could go even further and buy yourself a standard bay tree as an elegant and delightful-smelling reminder.

Bay is the 'true' laurel – other plants masquerading under the name are poisonous – and, to the Romans, it was a symbol of wisdom and glory. 'Laureate' means 'crowned with laurels; and, if we think of poets laureate, we think of creativity, balance and the ability to get their message across in a simple but deeply memorable way. Which describes your achievements perfectly.

Tread Softly

'I have spread my dreams under your feet:
Tread softly, because you tread on my dreams.'
W B Yeats, 1865-1939

If we have not yet moved into the Friendly Personal Aura, now is the time to pave the way; and, if we are already in Friendly Personal, we need to move as close to the Inner Core as possible. This is where the Intellectual and Psychological sub-auras come into play – at a personal, rather than a business, level. Friendly Personal involves sharing inner feelings and, to get close to the Inner Core, we may need to reveal a lot more of ourselves than we initially anticipated. One's most important job in Friendly Personal is as a listener: in this aura, people may want to share any worries and concerns they may have. And there are times when people may have worries and concerns which might seem completely crazy to us: imagine a phobia as an extreme example. Once again, this is a question of respect and acknowledgement: the phobia is very real to them, and this is what we are acknowledging. Or supposing they are being two-timed by someone we think is appalling anyway; their pain is very real, and we need to give it the respect it deserves. They're confiding in us because they trust us, and that's all there is to it.

So, why should we go to these lengths in a business context? Couldn't it be considered very unprofessional? And, anyway, isn't this verging on the touchy-feely? The simple answer is that, by revealing some of our inner-self, we demonstrate to the other party that we trust them with confidential information. Trust works both ways, and this can work wonders in many cultures.

Before we go any further, here are some questions:

1. Would I like to be confronted with a lawyer every time I close a deal?
2. Would my colleagues see me as inferior if I revealed some of my inner self?
3. Would the other party see me as inferior if I revealed some of my inner self?
4. Would I trust the other party?
5. Would I enjoy a long-term relationship with the other party?

If the answer to questions 1 is 'yes', be aware that sometimes lawyers have to be involved, particularly in the States; but, now that you are consciously aware that the presence of a lawyer annoys/offends you, you can accept that, be aware that other people think differently, and let it go. It's just a behaviour, after all; it is up to us to choose how we want to interpret it.

If you've answered 'yes' to 2 and 3, the question we would ask is 'how do you know?'

In other words, are you sure? Or have you made it up? What is your evidence that either your colleagues or the other party would see you as inferior, if you revealed some of your inner self? What do you see, hear, feel, taste and/or smell that proves to you that they would think of you as inferior? What hard evidence do you have? Or could you be mistaken?

If you are still uncertain about the safety of revealing more of yourself, play it carefully, and go with the flow. When the time seems appropriate, offer a relatively unimportant titbit, and see what response you get.

If the answers to questions 4 – 5 are 'no', again you need to be careful, unless of course you consider it useless to have a relationship with this person – in which case, forget it. If you trust the other guy, and would like to improve the relationship, we suggest you review the Formal and Friendly Business Auras, and how those have developed and are developing.

The purpose of moving closer to the Inner Core is that we're selling our selves; the business side of things is merely a complex intellectual transfer of personal data. The enhancement of our relationship can only be achieved by a follow-up.

We need only go back to the supplier we talked about at the beginning of the chapter, who's losing business to Diana's friend David, to assume that David's new customers like him much better than they like her. And, if we think of Sir John Harvey-Jones who, when he gives his friendship, gives it for life – and therefore cannot cope with people who wine and dine him until the contract is signed, and then disappear out of his life forever – we know which side of the fence we would rather be.

If we buy something from someone who makes us feel important, it is only reasonable to expect that they will continue to think we are important, and follow up on the sale to make sure we are happy with what we've got, with the service, and so on. If they drop us like hot cakes, we probably won't buy from them again.

The presuppositions of NLP

Things don't always work out the way we want or expect them to, and we may thank the Good Lord, in hindsight, that we didn't get a certain contract that we were after, because it turned out to be a can of worms for the people who did. Or we may sweat blood over a contract that we didn't really want – just as a matter of pride – which turned out not to be worth a hill of beans.

We've a lot talked about the Presuppositions of NLP and we thought it might be useful to list them here. Some of them we've covered, and some will just fit in to what we have been discussing. NL-People would never maintain that any of these is true, they are just a useful way of thinking and being in the world.

1. **The Map is not the Territory:** (borrowed from the authority on semantics, Alfred Korzybsky). We covered this fairly early on. Everyone has a different model of the world which they have created for themselves as a result of their experiences, culture, upbringing and so on. None of these maps is true, they are simply representations of the world as we know it. Therefore Bloggins's map of the world is just as valid as ours. It follows that if we have, quite properly, been brought up to believe that our nation is the greatest in the world, we are entitled to believe that the way we do things is 'the one right way'. And, if we have never been anywhere else in the world, it may never occur to us that there are other, just as efficient (and maybe better) ways of doing things.

2. **Life and mind are systemic processes:** we talked about this when we were covering negotiating. We are systems within systems: our brains affect our bodies, and our bodies affect our brains. It therefore follows that, if we are feeling bad, we are probably not going to perform at our best. This is why we advocate using your big, safe space when going into a situation which might make you feel nervous. If we feel safe, and good, we will be at our best, and also get the best from others in the system we are operating in at the time.

3. **The meaning of the communication is the response that you get:** if we omit to smile at someone, in a country where smiles are expected, they may think we are being deliberately rude, they may wonder what they have done wrong, they may think all sorts of things. The fact that our mind was on other things, and that the last thing we meant to do was to upset them, is irrelevant: ours was a non-smiling communication, and they have responded accordingly. Once again, this is an example of how we affect the system we are in.

4. **The most flexible part of any system is the one that will survive the longest:** we have also covered this. It is the Law of Requisite Variety from Cybernetics. In a hurricane, it is the supple willow trees that will survive by moving with the wind, and the solid oaks that will be toppled if they cannot give. This presupposition is invaluable in business.

5. **There is no failure, only feedback:** The story goes that, when Thomas Edison was asked how depressed he'd got by his 999 failures before he succeeded in making a light bulb that worked, he replied, indignantly: *'I didn't have 999 failures. I learned 999 ways how not to make a light bulb.'* Next time one of your projects doesn't go according to plan, ask yourself whether the first time you got onto a bicycle you just rode away – or whether it took time, and you learned from your mistakes how to get it right. It's just a question of asking ourselves what went wrong, and what we could have done differently. One way of doing this is to watch the whole thing over again on an imaginary television screen – simply replaying the video. Then we can see ourselves, as part of the system, and how we are affecting it.

6. **Every behaviour, however bizarre, has a positive intention:** there's endless mileage in this one if, for example, you're trying to make peace between warring parties who are banging on endlessly about the other side's behaviour. We all know people who behave aggressively when they feel a need to protect themselves, and fear creates perhaps the most off-putting behaviour. Our oldest brain is the reptilian brain, or brain stem, and its job is to keep us safe in the best way that it knows how; so, the moment if feels threatened, it will go into fight or flight mode. So, next time someone behaves aggressively towards you, you will know that all they need is to feel safe: expand your big safe space for them. In business, fear of the hierarchy, or just general fear of making a mistake, can make people unwilling to risk making a deal. But, if we remember that there is a positive intention behind it, we can explore this and discover what we can do to help.

7. **People make the best choices according to the information they have available to them at the time:** this may sound trite; but, when people are under pressure, their brains close down and they have no room to think or to manoeuvre. This is why some behaviour can appear completely bizarre. For example, have you ever known exactly what you

'should' do in a given situation – but blown it nonetheless?* Join the club: you're a member of the human race.

8. **People have within them all the resources that they need:** this one's a cracker. You will meet people who tell you that they've never, ever been able to stand up and speak in public. What resource do they need?, you ask them. Courage. So, go back to a time when you had courage, what did you see, hear, feel, taste and smell, when you had courage? Take all that with you, and make your presentation.

You can find out much more about these presuppositions in Diana's *Easy Being: Making Life as Simple and as Much Fun as Possible.* She wrote it because she was fed up with NLP's being sold as a series of surface-level tools and techniques, when it is infinitely more profound than that. You can get it via Amazon, through her website (see Bibliography).

Some more thoughts on values

Before we move on to the process of after-care, here is a little feedback exercise. You'll need a pencil and paper for each situation.

Intangible and/or abstract values	Tangible and/or concrete values
Integrity	Product or service quality
Honesty	Product or service presentation
Trust	Company presentation
Obsequiousness	Price
Straight talk	Financial rewards
Dress code	Payment terms
Relationship	Distribution
'We know better' attitude	Marketing elements including advertising

Table 11.1

*Books and training courses are great: they tell you *what* to do. This is fine for robots, but not completely useful for humans. The problem is, they don't tell you how to do it. If you take these presuppositions on board, you will find they give you a new and useful way of thinking that will give you the flexibility to respond usefully in difficult situations.

Think about your successes and the occasions when things have not gone according to plan, both for you and for other people; then look at Table 11.1, which consists of lists of both tangible and intangible values. Which were the most relevant and important values for both sides in each successful situation? And what were the least important?

Then think about the non-successful situations, and ask yourself the same questions. What differences do you notice?

In which aura do you do most of your business?	What are the most important intangible or abstract values?	What are the most important tangible or concrete values?
Formal Business Friendly Business Friendly Personal Inner Core		

Table 11.2 – Positioning Chart per country and per area, or even per person or company

We talk about modelling success, and here is your chance to model your own. Think about the times when you have been most successful doing business abroad, and ask yourself the questions in Table 11.2 (it would be helpful to give each situation a different chart because of the cultural differences, and so on). Take some time, and relive the meetings, and the negotiating. How long did you spend in Formal Business? Which aura were you in when you struck the deal? Are you still in touch with that person? Which aura are you in now?

Then move to the next column. Which were the most important intangible or abstract values involved in this piece of business? And then which were the most important tangible or concrete values?

By doing this, you will discover the structure of your own successes.

Once you have done that, you can think about the times when things didn't go according to plan, and fill in a chart for each occasion. What differences do you notice between the success and non-success charts? And, in particular, what was the change in the proportion of values from intangible to tangible on the occasions when things didn't work? This will give you an even clearer picture of what works for you,

You can use this chart for different countries, for different areas, for different companies, and even for different people to hone your skills to perfection. And, overall, you will discover that 99% of the time the intangible values are far more valuable.

The next interesting thing to do is to apply the 'success structure' to the non-successful occasions. In other words, we're going to reinvent the occasions that didn't work, and see what happens. Let's take your favourite success (A), and a situation that, in your opinion, went really badly (B).

- How were you feeling in Situation A? Light or heavy? Hot, cold, warm or cool? Stiff or supple?
- Was there stillness inside you, or movement?
- Was there an internal voice in your ear, or was it quiet?
- Did you feel your normal size, or did you feel small?
- Did you have the space to think and manoeuvre?

Then compare how you were feeling in Situation B. What differences do you notice in what you're experiencing in the two different situations?

Then think about the two other people involved.

- What was it that A did to make you feel the way you felt?
- What did person B do to make you feel the way you felt?

The next step is to take all the good stuff you were experiencing in situation A into situation B and re-run the movie in your imagination. What changes? Supposing that B says or does something that put you off last time, how do you respond this time when you're pretending that you feel safe and that you like B?

You'll find that everything happens quite differently; so the question now is: if that situation had gone this way, would you have got the deal?

Play around with this trick to explore other deals that have gone astray, and notice what you discover. Explore your past experience as many times as you want, until you feel so confident that you can walk into a meeting and have success 9 times out of 10. And, for that possible missing 10%, remember, we can't change the whole world, and – if it didn't work – it's probably because they were people you wouldn't want to do business with anyway.

Be careful what you ask for – you might just get it!

We need to be clear about what we want. This may seem self-evident, but you would be surprised at the number of people who blunder into a situation without being sure about what they want out of it. Here is a very simple exercise to make sure that you really want what you think you want. One of Diana's students, rather irreverently, called it 'The Christmas Tree' and the name has stuck.

Let's suppose that we want a Rolls Royce. Start at the bottom and work up.

Having discovered that what we want is really about more important things like confidence and happiness (and, as someone at one of Diana's workshops pointed out, that we all have the same sort of fairies at the top of our Christmas Trees), the next important question is to ask ourselves: *'what will we lose?'*

One thing we will certainly lose if we drive a Rolls is the ability to park

185

easily; it will also cost us a fortune to keep it on the road. If we are happy with these losses, then we can go ahead. If not, then we need to go up the tree to something more important: like 'confidence' in this case, and work out a different way of achieving that, without the collateral losses that go with our first wish.

Remembering that our outcome for our first business meeting is simply to establish the relationship and get an agreement to the second meeting, we can now do our Christmas Tree for the rest of the project. We want to get the business; so what will that give us, and what will we lose? For example, we now have sufficient knowledge of our opposite number to work out whether he or she is the sort of person we will enjoy doing business with, or whether they might turn out to be the customer from hell – in which case, will all the effort be worth our while, or the company's while?

The next important questions is: how will we know when we've got it? What will we see, hear, feel, taste and/or smell that will prove to us that we have achieved our outcome? In the case of the Rolls Royce, the answer is simple: we will have the car's log book, with our name as the registered owner of the vehicle. But how will we know when we have confidence? What does confidence look like, sound like, feel like, taste like, smell like?

> A friend of Diana's had a client whose outcome was to be rich. The problem was that he never defined, in his own mind, what 'rich' was, or what being rich would give him. He killed himself after the 1987 stock market crash, convinced that he would end up as a pauper. In fact, all he had lost was 25% of several billions, so he was still seriously rich; but, because he'd never thought through his outcomes properly, this fact passed him by.

If one of your outcomes is to be rich, how will you know when you've got it?

The whole outcomes exercise is very valuable, and it helps us to discover things that we didn't think we knew.

Outcomes for both parties

We can also use this exercise when we're negotiating, to get the best for both sides. Supposing the other company loves our widget, but cannot afford our bottom price. Once again, start at the bottom and work up.

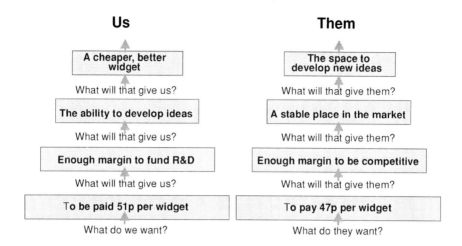

If we both insist on our first outcomes:

- **What will we lose?** A potentially very good customer, with a high-quality product.
- **What will they lose?** A high-quality widget

However, having done our outcomes exercise, we realise that we both want to develop new ideas: we need the money and they need the space. So this is a level at which we could co-operate to the advantage of both sides.

Going back to our previous discussions on negotiating, and the fact that our colleague may have his or her own agenda, we can do this outcomes exercise with them, for what they want for themselves, running it in parallel with what they want for their company.

One final question

Do you believe in your product? We ask this because, as sure as eggs is eggs, if you don't believe in it, then your new colleague won't believe in it either. As we have already discovered, the unconscious mind picks everything up and, however convincing your argument may seem, if you don't believe in what you're saying, it will come across as flawed.

In one of Diana's workshops, she paired people up and sent them off to sell a brilliant product to each other. At the end of the exercise, they were asked: *'would you buy this product?'*, and the answer was a unanimous 'yes'. For the second half of the exercise, she told the sales people that what they were to sell was a load of rubbish, but they still had to go for it. This time, the answer to the *'would you buy this product?'* question was a unanimous 'no'.

The next question was: *'what did you notice that was different about the sales people from the way they came across in the first part?'* Lots of things came up, but one woman said: 'nothing'. Diana was somewhat surprised, and asked for more information. It transpired that Sam, who was the designated salesman had said, up front: *'this is a load of rubbish'*. He'd remained true to himself, so there was no difference in the unconscious signals he was giving out.

Diana was once asked to sit in on a Sales Training course, and heard endless people giving utterly forgettable presentations: even at the end of the course, when they'd been taught all the things they 'should' do, she wouldn't have spent a penny on any of their products. When she asked one of the participants, as a matter of interest, whether he believed in whatever it was, he looked completely astonished. Passion had simply not been brought into the equation.

Try this on some colleagues: tell them you are going to sell them a second-hand car, and get them to close their eyes. Tell them that there are three cars to choose from: A, B and C. And then, using the same phrase, which could be: 'I've got just the car for you', take on three different physiologies:

(a) with your arms folded
(b) leaning forward, obsequiously rubbing your hands
(c) standing up straight and balanced, with your hands open.

Just use your normal voice for all three. If necessary, repeat the exercise if your colleagues want to hear it again. You will find that most of them will choose car C, because your physiology will have affected their decision – even though they had their eyes closed, they will pick up how your physiology affects your message.

The easy way to become passionate about your product is to know all its strengths and possible weaknesses – so that you can live it, breathe it and be it (when appropriate). The simple way to do this is to lay out a 'logical levels' line on the ground and walk it, stopping in each spot, and asking ourselves the questions:

➔ Where and when is it useful?
➔ What does it do?

→ How does it do it?
→ Why we need it?
→ Who am I, in relation to it?
→ Who does benefit?
→ Who else will it benefit?
→ How does it/will it benefit the planet?

As the answers to each question come to you, breathe them in, and lift and energise your physiology.

By doing this exercise physically, on the ground, we get the whole concept into our bodies and, when we do, we are engaged, aligned and committed. Everything we say and do comes across as congruent with the message we want to get across.

Persistence, flexibility and honesty with ourselves is all we need: success is not only in our own minds, it is also in our bodies.

Success Checklist

1. You've come a long way, and done a good job. Reward yourself.

2. Now's the time to prepare the ground for moving into Friendly Personal, or - if already there - towards the Inner Core.

3. Keep the presuppositions of NLP in mind at all times.

4. The intangible values are the most important and the most powerful.

5. Model your own successes.

6. Work out: what you want, how you will know when you've got it, and what you will lose - and amend your outcome, if necessary.

7. Have passion for your product!

8. Success is not only in your mind, it is also in your body.

9. Persistence, flexibility and honesty with yourself is all you need.

12

The Question of After Care

We've done it! We've got the business!

So now it's time to pack up and go home after all our hard work, isn't it?

WRONG! This is just the end of the beginning: and the second part of our work starts now. The one thing we are not going to do is to leave our new friends high and dry. We've promised to supply them with a product, and it's now up to us to ensure that that supply goes exactly according to plan; and that they feel supported and appreciated throughout the time we do business together.

If it can go wrong, it will

In *Steps to an Ecology of Mind*, Gregory Bateson has a number of meta-conversations with his daughter, one of which is entitled *'Daddy, Why do Things get in a Muddle?'* To answer her question, he goes round her room moving things an inch or so away from where she'd put them; and, in response to the horrified *'No, Daddy, that's not right'*, demonstrates that there is an infinity of places that are 'not right' according to her system of placement, compared with the one place that is 'right' – so it is all too easy for things to get into a muddle.

When things go wrong, even thought it may be through no fault of our own, our customer needs someone to contact, who will be sympathetic and who will sort it out.

Paperwork!

When Diana asked James McGlashan, the MD of Autoroute Total Logistics why she should use his company to ship her stuff to the States, rather than do it herself, the response was: *'Of course you can do it yourself, if you want to; but it will all go horribly wrong because you won't understand the paperwork.'* Shipping stuff abroad means coming up against the other country's protection systems: and every country has different protection systems, which all involve reams of paper and seemingly endless rules. We need to employ a professional if we don't want to waste our and our customer's time.

Diana hitched a lift back to Germany from Iran, in a lorry. As they approached the Turkish border crossing, they found queues of stationary lorries stretched for miles and miles. Fortunately, they had an agent travelling with them, so they were allowed to join a separate queue and only had to wait for four hours; but, later in the journey, they met agentless drivers who had had to queue for three or four days in order to get through customs. The agent was Iranian, and he knew what was what. Apart from having the paperwork right, he was part of that culture and knew how to handle not only the Iranian customs officials, but also those on the Turkish side.

If we're shipping goods abroad, life without an agent is not worth the hassle.

The other thing we need to think about is distributors, if – having gained a foothold – we want to promote our product throughout the country in question.

Life with distributors and agents

If we're going to employ distributors and agents, they are going to be the main link between our customers and us, so we need to make sure that they are going to continue to build on the relationship: if they do this, they can act as brilliant boosters to our business; if they don't, all our good work may fizzle away to nothing.

On the whole, distributors or agents are local people, but this is not necessarily so; alternatively they may represent our company in one or several countries. Therefore when we are choosing who is going to act for us, we need to ask ourselves one of these questions:

- Do they understand the local population in the area they work in?

or

- Do they understand the population in the different countries they work in?

We're looking for distributors who are going to be active, and who will put in a lot of effort to sell our products or services, rather than the passive version who are only interested in products and services, which sell themselves; and, in Ron's experience there are considerably more in the second group than there are in the first. In the second group, we'll find distributors who are only interested in the margins they receive at the end of the day, without putting much effort into achieving their goals. This will only result in customers contacting us on a daily basis trying to do business directly, which is not the object of the exercise.

When we're deciding upon a distributor or an agent for a particular area, there are two sets of questions we need to ask ourselves, first about the tangible and secondly about the intangible aspects of their service.

Some examples of tangible aspects:

- Are they financially trustworthy?
- Have they got the necessary assets, buildings, offices, transport, warehouse, etc?

As we saw in earlier chapters, it is the intangible aspects that matter to us, and the key questions here are:

1. Do they understand the local culture?
2. Do they understand the local market?
3. Do they understand the local way of doing business?
4. Are they interested in representing our company as if it were theirs?
5. Are they good listeners?
6. Are they qualified to represent our products/services?
7. Are they good communicators?
8. Do they have the appropriate approach to represent our company?
9. Are they open to suggestions?
10. Are they proactive?
11. Are they willing to achieve?
12. Are they the sort of people we want to have a close relationship with?

Let's look at these points in more detail.

1. Do they understand the local culture?

If they are natives, they will. If they are not natives, we need to find out what the natives think of them.

2. Do they understand the local market?

In Ron's experience, some distributors and agents have little or no understanding of local markets, or who their potential customers are, and may even have little or no idea what the market is. This is especially true in countries which were deprived of such an education. For instance in some Middle Eastern and former East European countries as well as in the former Soviet Union, people may have little to no understanding of these aspects.

However, they might be very willing to learn; and, if they're keen, we can train them up accordingly, in market surveys, marketing and sales. In fact, it might even be better to work with people like this rather than those who claim they know it all.

As an example of the above, when Ron first met his distributors in Iran they had little knowledge of the market, or of marketing or even of sales. On the other hand they were very well educated in the science, which was necessary to understand his products. Also, they were extremely eager to learn. So he trained them and the result was a great success.

3. Do they understand the local way of doing business?

This of course is essential. Do they understand how to approach business people in their own area? Do they act according to CAT and NLP, as explained in previous chapters? (All right, so they haven't read this book yet, but are they aware of which aura they need to be in, and how to get there, before they start to talk business, in their particular area?) Do they relate to people as individuals? Or do they act as if all customers are the same?

Once again, we can train these people up, as long as they are willing to learn. They may follow the CAT system without knowing what it is about, but it is essential that they have an in-depth understanding of relationship-building whether consciously or unconsciously.

Interestingly, when Ron has offered to train people, they have been delighted, because they could use what they had learned to improve their own overall business.

Figure 13.1 explains how we can use the IOTM model for working with distributors or agents.

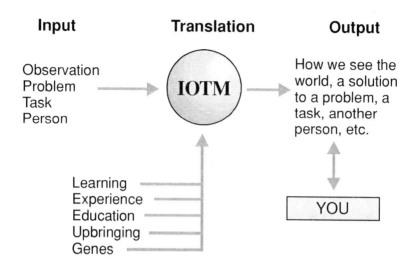

Fig 13.1 – IOTM for distributors or agents

Once again, we are looking for a solution to suit everybody. We can compare their IOTM with ours, and observe how they solve a problem or task in relation to the way that we do. If we then discuss the differences with them, and how we would handle the situation using CAT and NLP, we can come up with an output which satisfies everyone.

4. Are they interested in representing our company as if it were theirs?

The image of our company needs to be conveyed to their customers. We all know of companies which have such an excellent image that, when we buy their goods, they have to be good by definition. We do not even question the fact that these products may not be the best, and are blissfully unaware that we can buy the identical product under another company's banner at half the price.

We want our distributor to represent our company's image, and the important question here is: are the images of the two companies compatible? Do they represent the same values? Will they be able to promote our product from the heart, with passion, because our product fits in with their image?

If ours is a newly-created company, then the image will need to be built in the new country. Has this distributor got the potential to do this? Or might it be better to work with a longer-established distributor whose image is already rock solid?

One key factor in image-building is customer service. Many companies, or people, or even nations, have little notion of customer service, which varies from promptly replying to e-mails and telephone calls, to ensuring that goods are delivered on time; and it relates particularly to trouble-shooting action and acknowledging mistakes.

Once again this can be taught and a distributor who is not used to providing good customer service may prefer to be guided along these lines, rather than be left to cope on their own. And, if we can find a distributor with a good reputation for customer services, we're in luck.

5. Are they good listeners?

In all fairness, we are all guilty of not paying proper attention from time to time. Nonetheless it is impossible to underestimate the importance of listening: if we don't listen, the other person feels unimportant, and disrespected. Our distributor's job is to make our customers feel as though they are the only other person in the world, at that moment.

Ron once visited a customer with two representatives of his company's distributors. One was a sales guy, and the other was a scientist.

The sales guy presented the company first, and then the scientific person did his bit. The customer, who probably wasn't a scientist, got bored with all the jargon and said: *'I want you to answer my question, how do you put this into practice?'*

Rather than responding to a question he couldn't answer by referring the questioner to Ron or the sales guy, the scientist started rabbiting on about something completely irrelevant.

Not acknowledging the question simply demonstrated a lack of respect – unforgivable in any circumstances; and, had it been a more difficult question, which none of them could answer, he could simply have promised to find out, which would have not only honoured the questioner's perspicacity, but also achieved the outcome of providing the answer, albeit at a later date..

6. Are they qualified to represent our products/services?

This may seem a very basic question, but it is an aspect which sometimes gets forgotten.

Our distributor needs to understand our products or services as well as we do. They need to be able to relate to customers and explain them from A to Z, including all their strengths and weaknesses. We cannot assume that, because they handle similar products to ours that they will do a good job for us: it's our unique product that we are talking about.

One way of testing this out is to visit some customers together, to get a feel for how they handle our product, and how they get the message across.

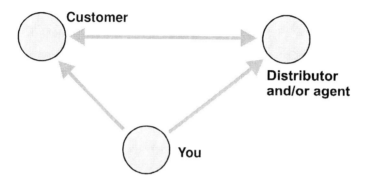

Fig 12.2 – How we perceive the other parties

The official reason for this visit is to act as support for our new distributor; we will let him or her do the presentation, and simply be there in case there are questions that he or she cannot answer. We can then act as observer – see Figure 12.2 – and see from the outside how our distributor comes across to our prospective customer, and the customer's perception of our distributor – which might be quite different from ours. And the questions are: does this relationship work? And is our distributor getting the message across in the way we would like him to, and according to our values?

7. Are they good communicators?

In business, as in life, communication is the be all and end all. The whole business of keeping the system that is life alive, is the buying and selling of ideas. We don't buy products; we buy intangible concepts like people, ideas and values.

Therefore, in order to represent us, our distributor needs to be a good communicator. He needs to have the skills to be able to sell his personality, his concepts and his intangible assets to willing buyers. The art of communication is to convey a message about a concept in such a way that the other party will want to buy into it.

When Ron was working for a large American multi-national, he used to send his scientific people on sales trainings. Why? Because it was the scientists who had the ideas, and it was they who had to sell their ideas to Ron, in the first place, before these ideas could be developed – quite apart from selling them to the customers later.

Scientists are trained as scientists, not as sales people; and they can get so wrapped up in their own technical auras that it may never occur to them that others don't think the same way as they do – to wit, the scientist we met above, who droned on and on with his story, and didn't answer the prospective customer's question.

It's just a question of augmenting their own technical auras with another technical aura (sales), which can only enrich their work and their lives.

8. Do they have the appropriate approach to represent our company?

We're not talking about financial means or human resources, but rather their attitude towards business. Do they think along the same lines as we do? Have they got the same values as we have: in other words, are they prepared to build long term relationships with our clients. Have they got the means to train their people according to our standards? Or have they already got people with whom we can work without problems?

If we are thinking in terms of a collection of several individuals, rather than one person, we need to ensure that all the people involved understand how we think, and how we want the distributorship/s to operate.

A distributor may not be a single person but a collection of several individuals. We need then to identify that the people involved have the understanding of all the aspects discussed in this chapter.

9. Are they open to suggestions?

Our distributors need to be able to create hybrid paradigms to satisfy all three parties. (See figure 12.3 opposite.) If they are local, they are more likely to lean towards the customer's paradigm; so they need to be aware of what will and what won't work for us as well. Getting them versed in our way of doing business, in order to achieve this, may well be a complex exercise, but it will be well worth it!

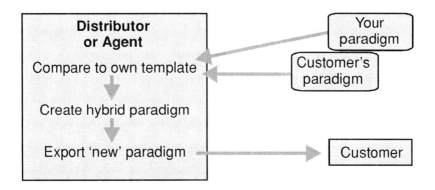

Fig 12.3 – The distributor's hybrid paradigm

10. Are they proactive?

Are they able to foresee what needs to be done, in advance, rather than reacting to problems as they arise?

The world is changing so rapidly that products and services may need to be adapted accordingly. Whole businesses may need to adapt. Have they got the wit and intelligence to foresee and adapt to these changes, including changes to our own input?

11. Are they willing to achieve?

Most people are very willing to achieve, as there is always an incentive. This may not be necessarily a financial one; it may well be one of status or purely personal. It might be worth sitting down with them, and taking them through the logical levels, to discover what they really want from life.

We would also suggest doing the parallel Christmas Trees exercise, to ensure that our distributor's outcomes can be achieved as well as ours – making sure that our distributor has a clear idea of what his evidence will be as he achieves his outcomes along the way.

Doing this makes the distribution into a true joint, and therefore much more valuable, venture.

12. Are they the sort of people we want to have a strong relationship with?

Our relationship with our distributors and agents needs to be just as strong as it is with our customers – if not stronger. So, unless the answer to this question is 'yes', we need to look for someone else.

Success will depend upon how we interact with our distributors or agents. People enjoy passing on their wisdom, and learning from other people's wisdom. We have a lot to learn from a distributor on the ground; so on the one hand we can be the students, and on the other, the teachers. Creating a good balance of the two will stimulate our distributors' interest in working with us, to achieve both their goals and ours. They will feel proud that they can teach us, and they will also enjoy learning from us – to the benefit of both parties.

While they are learning, they are likely to make mistakes, and these mistakes may cause us some aggravation. So here are two of the NLP presuppositions that will be useful here.

- **Every behaviour, however bizarre has a positive intention**; in other words, they didn't make the mistake on purpose, so it's just a question of finding out how it happened.

- **The meaning of the communication is the response that you get**: that is to say, if we told them to do something, and they didn't do it, we obviously didn't get our message across properly.

It's also useful to think about the logical levels of criticism, so that both sides are quite clear that the equation: the fact that X's order hasn't arrived does not mean that Y is an idiot.

- Where and when did the mistake happen?
- What happened?
- How did it happen?
- Has this mistake got anything to do with who Y is?

People are very inclined to criticise others at identity level, in other words, using the verb 'to be' followed by an adjective, for example ...

- you are incompetent
- he is irresponsible
- she is arrogant
- they are a bunch of idiots

... when, in fact, the problem was caused by a behaviour, or maybe a lack of capability, and has nothing to do with who the person is. This kind of criticism is endemic – we only have to listen to children, who have copied their parents and their teachers, to realise how and why people do it.

Grammatically, it can only be interpreted at identity level, so it's no wonder that people grow up feeling worthless and inadequate – unless they've managed to work out the logical levels for themselves.

People love logical levels, once they've got the hang of them: teach them to your distributors, they'll appreciate it.

Two delightful 12-year old French children, who weren't getting on very well at school, came to spend some time with Diana. They spent a day at a Jemima Parry-Jones's falconry, watching assorted birds being flown by different trainers. The next day, they put it all on the computer:
- where and when each bird hunted
- what each bird hunted
- how each bird hunted
- why each bird hunted in the way that it did
- who each bird was.

And it was at that point that they said, by way of a huge discovery: *'that's why Jemima is such a good trainer! She treats each bird as an individual!'* (Jemima is very good and very well-known.)

One of the mothers came to collect them, and addressed an identity level criticism to her daughter: *'you are untidy'* – or something; and the 12-year old Caroline leaned nonchalantly against the sofa, grinned at Diana and said: *'I wonder what logical level I'll choose to take that criticism at.'*

The mother rang Diana later, and said that she'd had 'logical levels all the way home.'

And while you're about it, why not join Diana's franchise: every time that anyone who works with you uses the words 'should' or 'ought to' about somebody else, they owe you £5. And, every time they used either of them about themselves, they owe you £50. 'Should' and 'ought to' are terrible words. They make the speaker out to be superior; and, if the speaker is superior, what does that make the other person in the loop?

The £50 fine is for treating yourself badly. If you treated your staff the way that you treat yourself, how long would they stay with you? Your self has looked after you since the day you were born, and deserves at least as much respect, support, acknowledgement and love as you give other people.

Obviously we will continue to monitor and help our distributors, while they are finding their feet, and we will also need to be there as mentors for them, for as long as they need us, while giving them the freedom to grow into the job and blossom. So what is the true meaning of the word mentor?

When the young Telemachus went off in search of his father, Ulysses, Minerva – the goddess of wisdom – went with him, in human form, as his guide, wise counsellor and faithful friend, Mentor.

Happy Partnership!

Success Checklist

1. Keep the customers feeling happy and supported.
2. If it can go wrong it will: have someone there to field the problems.
3. Paperwork is for the professionals.
4. Ask the twelve questions about possible distributors.
5. Is this prospective distributor someone you want to have a long term relationship with?
6. A Mentor is a guide, wise counsellor or friend.
7. Treat your self at least as well as you treat your staff.

13

The Travelling Business Companion

Before you start this chapter, we suggest you go back to the Chartres labyrinth on page 83, and trace its path again with the index finger of your left hand. This will rebalance all the information you have received since you last did it, and set you up to draw your own conclusions, as well as ours.

Our plan for this book was to provide you with a companion to be at your side from the moment you know you have to go abroad on business until you have concluded your deal, and beyond – into a long-term, fruitful business relationship – with each relationship adding to your network of world-wide business colleagues who will be useful to you for the rest of your life.

Our theory is simple: each person we deal with is a unique individual, with his or her own complex nature, inside his or her culture. And, because every person we work with really matters to us, we enjoy his or her unique spectrum of cultural values and enter into them with pleasure.

The surface-level impressions that we have given you in the chapter 'How we see the Others' are just our impressions, and there is absolutely no guarantee that people will behave in the way we suggest. They are who they are, and they do things their way. (For more in-depth studies of different nations and their cultures, see the bibliography.)

So, in conclusion:

Time spent in reconnaissance is never wasted

The more research we can do into the culture and environment of the country we are about to visit, the better we will get on. And, if we can research the company, its culture and its people as well, so much the better.

The two magic words: Culture and Relationship

We've talked a lot about values, both abstract and concrete; and, although a business that doesn't pay attention to its bottom line may not succeed, business is all about people. Neither culture nor relationships has any concrete value but, if we don't give them both our full attention, we are lost if we're going to try to do business abroad.

We do things our way; they do things theirs

There's more than one right way of doing things. We can enjoy using our creativity to create a solution to suit both parties. And, who knows, maybe we will learn some new, and more efficient, ways of doing things from our new business partners and colleagues.

The Cultural Auras Theory

CAT provides you with a new toolbox whereby you can calculate how various cultures like to do business, so that you can enter their model of the world and do things their way; this not only honours and respects their culture, it also gives you a much greater chance of success.

CAT is simply a structure, and you can apply it to any situation you may find yourself in, in your own unique style; what is more, you can find your own ways to amend and improve upon it, so that it fits in entirely with your way of thinking. It's yours to do what you like with.

NLP

NLP is just another structure: this time for thinking. Its two most powerful facets for the Business Chameleon are probably Logical Levels and the Presuppositions. You can use the Logical Levels to ask yourself what level both you and the other person are thinking and whether this is the relevant level for the situation; and, if you take the presuppositions on board, you will find yourself able to maintain your equilibrium whatever other people may throw at you.

Some questions to ask

As we move into Friendly Business, it's often entertaining and useful to ask our prospective colleague what it is about us, i.e. our nation, that (a) they like, (b) bewilders them and (c) drives them mad. The answers can be every revealing, both for us – and for them, as we explain why it is that we behave in a particular way. It also gives us the chance to avoid, if we can, doing the things that drive them mad. And, if the relationship is going well, they might ask us the same questions, to reach a deeper level of understanding.

A question for you

What are you doing on the planet? In other words, what difference is your being on the planet making and going to make to it? For example, doing effective business with another country helps to create cross-cultural understanding, which can only be a good thing. Make yourself a list of your contributions to the good of the planet, and then add any further contributions you would like to make. Doing this gives you a clearer idea of where you are going, and where you want to go; and, once you have done it, you'll be surprised at how things begin to fall into place.

A last question for you

If you treated your prospective colleagues the way you treat yourself, would they want to do business with you? In our experience, most people treat others with respect, kindness and courtesy, and treat themselves disgracefully: they are always niggling away at themselves about not being good enough, and so on – which is no way to treat anybody. So, the only serious injunction that we are going to give you is: *Trust Your Self*. Your self knows all this stuff anyway. How often, while reading this book have you thought: 'I knew that'; or 'I could have worked that out for myself'; or 'that's just common sense'? And, with this trust, come all the other things we give our friends, like acknowledgement, thanks, consideration, generosity and so on; in other words, treat your self at least as well as you treat others, and notice how the relationship changes.

Resonance

As a result of having read your way through this book, you may be thinking that, next time you go abroad on business, you will have to keep so many balls in the air at the same time that your whole act could fall apart. Or you could be thinking that you now have such a feel for different cultures that you can fit in anywhere.

The trick is resonance: compare the sounds of African and Western choirs. In Western choirs, we have tenors and basses, sopranos and contraltos, among others, each singing their own parts; whereas, in African choirs, everyone just sings the notes they know will resonate with the rest of the voices. In other words, we can still be ourselves, because we already have the resonance with our new colleagues at the heart level; and, with this kind of resonance, we will know instinctively how to fit into any situation.

A small example of this: English gentlemen don't kiss hands (like the French) or click their heels (like the Germans) when they meet a lady. It is an accepted fact among the French and Germans that, unless one learned how to do it at one's mother's knee, one will have no class or style and will just look stupid. So the Englishmen say all the right things, behave as they would in polite society in England, and stand out less like sore thumbs than they would if they attempted to do what does not come naturally to them. Adapt where you can without making a fool of yourself.

Another illustration: Diana got into a complete panic before going to live in France – her husband was to be the British Liaison Officer at the French Cavalry School, where things haven't changed much since the 18th Century. Good manners, she felt sure would be of the highest priority, and she had no idea about French manners. Her opposite number in England came to her rescue. *'There are only two things that the English need to know about living in France:'* she said. *'1. There will always be salt and pepper on the dinner table; never help yourself to it: you will imply that the cooking is not perfect; and 2. Never ask to go to the loo in someone else's house. Any other mistakes that you make will be anglaises, and therefore adorables!'* Both Beavers abode rigidly by these rules, were gathered into the bosom by the French, made some wonderful friends and had a fabulous two and a half years.

People are very forgiving of foreigners, as a matter of principle. There is nothing they would like more than to be able to accept you for who you really are.

Some thoughts on jazz

As we write this, the news has come through of the death of the skiffle singer Lonnie Donnegan. You are probably far too young to remember him, but he brought a whole new concept of music into the pop charts, which lasted until the arrival of the Beatles. John Peel, the disc jockey, said of Donnegan that, because of his jazz background, every time he sang a song, it was different; and that, once the Beatles arrived, things sadly changed and everyone sang their songs exactly the same every time.

The point of this metaphor is that we would like you to go out and improvise: sing every song differently, adapting it to your audiences – rather than expecting your audiences to adapt to you. (Interestingly, Diana has just discovered that her friend Michael Bochmann, the eminent violinist, is writing a book on exactly this subject – relating to the modern interpretation of classical music. His feeling is that musicians are concentrating on playing perfectly as individuals – which comes across as mechanical – instead of including the rest of the orchestra and the audience in their performance, and making each performance an unforgettable event for everyone.)

And Lonnie Donnegan had such fun – as did everyone who enjoyed his songs.

All this leaves us wondering when the shift began in business from gentlemen's agreements to phalanxes of lawyers, and when high-level sport stopped being fun and became deadly earnest – in other words, when money became more important than relationships.

It's not what you know, it's who you know

When Ron decided to set up his own company, he looked through the 2,000 odd business cards in his files. These were not just cards he'd picked up from strangers: they were all friends with whom he'd done business throughout the years. He sent out his prospectus to a selected six of these people, and the work came pouring in.

It is extremely important to build up a sound network and to savour it at all times.

Where to start networking? There are numerous possibilities to identify leads throughout this world: from the simple yellow pages to, for instance, *The European Public Affairs Directory* to name just two. The list is endless: trade journals, professional and trade associations, chambers of commerce, embassies, universities, international organisations, competitors, and many more.

One thing is for sure – always keep contact with anyone within your network and never underestimate a lead.

This book is for you

Keep it with you whenever you travel abroad, so that you have always got it to refer to, and so that you can add to the notes you have made. Take what you find in it, play with it and explore both other cultures and your self. Develop what you've learned, and use what you have discovered, and continue to discover, to get a better understanding of all the people you are going to be meeting and dealing with in the future.

Above all, have fun with it, and always remember that it takes all sorts to make a world, and that we would never want to put people into boxes.

We hope you have enjoyed reading it as much as we enjoyed writing it – we learned so much from each other, and only had one argument: Diana wanted RM Associates (Ron's company) to do something for her. They gave her a quote, and did the job perfectly. But it became abundantly clear that it had cost far more than the quote. Diana wanted to pay more, but Ron wasn't having it: they had given their quote, it was a question of honour, and that was that.

And last but not least, may we wish you all the success you deserve in your foreign endeavours. May you thoroughly enjoy all your new discoveries, and may all your new discoveries and your new friends enrich your life.

Bibliography and Tapes

These book can be ordered hassle-free from the Amazon of your choice via Diana's website: **http://www.dianabeaver.co.uk**.

Andreas, Steve & Connirae: *Change Your Mind – And Keep the Change*, Real People Press, USA, 1987: *The Heart of the Mind*, Real People Press, USA, 1989

Bandler, Richard, and Grinder, John: *Frogs into Princes*, Real People Press, USA, 1979

Bandler, Richard: *Using Your Brain – for a Change*, Real People Press, USA, 1985: *Time for a Change*, Meta Publications, USA, 1993

Bateson, Gregory: *Steps to an Ecology of Mind*, Jan Aronson, Inc, USA, 1972: *Mind and Nature*, Bantam Books, 1988

Beaver, Diana: *Easy Being: Making Life as Simple and as Much Fun as Possible*, Useful Book Company, 1997: *NLP for Lazy Learning*, Vega Books, 2002

Bryson, Bill: *Mother Tongue*, Penguin, 1991: *Notes from a Small Island*, Black Swan, 1996: *Notes from a Big Country*, Black Swan, 1999

Carlzon, Jan: *Moments of Truth: New Strategies for Today's Custom Driven Economy*, Harper & Row, 1989

Daninos, Pierre: *Les Carnets du Major Thompson*, Hachette, 1954

Dilts, Robert: *Changing Belief Systems with NLP*, Meta Publications, 1990: *Skills for the Future*, Meta Publications, 1993

Eicher, James: *Making the Message Clear*, Metamorphous Press, USA, 1987

Faulkner, Charles; Mc Donald, Robert; Hallbom, Tim and Smith Suzi: *NLP: The New Technology for Achievement*, UK and USA, Simon & Schuster Audio, UK and USA, 1993

Financial Times: *World Desk Reference*, Dorling Kindersley, UK, 2000

Fisher, Roger & Ury, William: *Getting to Yes*, Hutchinson Business, 1981

Garfield, Simon: *Mauve*, Faber and Faber, UK, 2000

Goleman, Daniel: *Emotional Intelligence*, Audio Renaissance Tapes, UK, 1995

Hall, E.T. *The silent language*. Garden City, NY: Anchor Press/Doubleday, 1959: *Beyond culture*, Garden City, NY: Anchor Press/Doubleday, 1977: *The dance of life*, Garden City, NY: Anchor Press/Doubleday, 1983: *Hidden Differences: Studies in International Communication*, Hamburg: Gruner & Jahr, 1985: *Hidden differences: Doing business with the Japanese*, Garden City, NY: Anchor Press/Doubleday. 1987: *Understanding cultural differences*, Yarmouth, ME: Intercultural Press, 1990

Hampden-Turner, Charles: *Corporate Culture*, The Economist Books, UK, 1990

Hayes, Nicky: *Psychology*, Hodder & Stoughton, UK, 1994

Hill, Richard: *We Europeans*, Europublications, Belgium, 1995

Hofstede, Geert: *Cultures and organisations*, Harper Collins, UK, 1994

Jacobson, Sid: *Solution States,: A Course of Solving Problems in Business with the Power of NLP*, Anglo American Book Company, 1996

Laborde, Genie: *Influencing with Integrity*, Anglo-American Book Company, 1997

Lewis, Richard D: *When Cultures Collide*, Nicholas Brealey, UK, 2000

Lynn, Jonathan & Jay, Anthony: *Yes, Minister*, BBC Publications, 1989: *Yes, Prime Minister*, BBC Publications, 1986

McMaster, Michael & Grinder, John: *Precision: A New Approach to Communication*, Precision Models, 1980

Mikes, George: *How to be an Alien*, Penguin, 1999

Miller, Lawrence M: *Barbarians to Bureaucrats*, Random House Audio Publishing, Canada, 1989

Miyashita, Kenichi; Russell, David: *Keiretsu*, McGraw-Hill, USA, 1994

Morris, Desmond: *Manwatching*, Triad, Panther, 1978: *Gestures*, Jonathan Cape, 1979

Peters, Tom and Austin, Nancy: *A Passion for Excellence*, Warner Books, USA, 1986

Peters, Tom: *Thriving on Chaos*, Alfred A. Knopf, Inc, USA, 1987: *Liberation Management*, Alfred A. Knopf, Inc, USA, 1992

Rowland, Diana: *Japanese Business Etiquette*, Warner Books, UK, 1994

The European Public Affairs Directory, Landsmark SA/NV, 2003 (published annually)

Toffler, Alvin: *The Third Wave*, London, Pan Books, UK, 1981

Watts, David: *Guide to Japan*, Times Books, UK, 1993

Zarro, Richard A & Blum, Peter: *The Phonebook: Neurolinguistic Skills for Profit and Enlightenment*, Metamorphous Press, 1989

For *Living Values*, go to: http://.livingvalues www.net

Invest in People and your business will be fun and profitable

General Business/Management Development

Strategy and Vision Development
- Drafting and inplementation of customer-tailored and innovative business strategies

Market and Geographical Expansion
- Analysis of present and future markets
- Identifying optimum marketing and sales channels
- Identifying business partners
- Identifying distributors

Innovative Product Management
- Identifying innovative products
- Acquisition
- In-house development
- Exterior development

Marketing and Sales Strategies Management
- Drafting and implementation of customer-tailored marketing and sales action plans
- Innovative and revolutionary marketing tools
- Customer-relationship management

International Business/Management Development and Training using its unique CAT technique - The Art of Achieving Success in Business Abroad

Business Development abroad
- Coping with cultural differences

International Management
- Overall management skills
- Managing people skills
- Managing distributor skills
- Preparing the new grounds
- Launching new venture abroad

Marketing and Sales Management
- Marketing and sales skills including negotiations techniques and concluding deals
- Presentation skills
- Export skills

Legislation and Regulations
- Overcoming hurdles abroad

**CAT technique developed by Ron Roet, MD,
and endorsed by Henley Management College, UK**

RM Associates Ltd.
28-30 Cecily Hill, Cirencester, Glos., GL7 2EF, UK
Tel: +44 1285 658 508 Fax: +44 1285 658 597 Mobile:
+44 7789 724 060 Email: ron.roet@rmassociatesltd.com

people solutions
Diana Beaver

BUSINESS SERVICES
Communication for people at the sharp end
Dealing with difficult people
Presenting your real self
The F word (what's stopping you?)
The patent Beaver method for dealing with stress
Personal consultancy for senior management

BENEFITS

Customers/clients feel that they matter
A happier workforce
Increased business
Increased productivity
Less stress-related absenteeism,
Time-out for clarity of thinking and vision

PERSONAL SERVICES

One-to-one for: relationships, difficult people, learning, sport, self-confidence,
stress, health, performance, post-traumatic stress

BENEFITS

You'll make life simpler, feel better, achieve what you want to achieve, have
more time and have more fun

Contact Diana Beaver
telephone: 01451 850863
website: www.dianabeaver.co.uk